BYGONE BARBADOS

ANN WATSON YATES

Published by

BLACK BIRD STUDIOS

Montclere, Lodge Hill Wood, Lodge Hill,
St. Michael, Barbados
Tel: (246) 435-7078

First published 1998
Second Printing 1999

ISBN: 976-8077-64-6

Printed in Barbados by Cole's Printery Limited

This book is dedicated to Peter Allard
with affection and gratitude.
Quite simply, without him
it would not have been possible.

PETER ALLARD

I had hoped that Dr Karl Watson
would write this book, unfortunately due
to prior commitments he was unable to do so.
Nevertheless he was always there to encourage me,
to control my excesses and to put at my disposal his knowledge
of the diverse subjects covered by this book and
I cannot thank him enough for his academic input.

Karl is indeed a true academic and the main purpose of his life
has been to seek and share knowledge.
He is totally without pettiness,
selfishness or meanmindedness; rare qualities,
especially in academic life.

One of my great pleasures is that he
happens to be my cousin.

DR KARL WATSON

Acknowledgements

My husband *ALAN* for his help, support and tolerance during the writing of this book.

HENRY FRASER, SEAN CARRINGTON, ADDINTON FORDE and *JOHN GILMORE,* whose book "A—Z of Barbadian Heritage" was absolutely invaluable and from which I have quoted extensively.

MR B. FERGUSSON, KARL WATSON, PETER ALLARD, HENRY FRASER, MRS N. PATTERSON, MARY GREEN, COL. CAVE for the use of photographs from their collections.

CAMBRIDGE UNIVERSITY PHOTO LIBRARY who did not charge for the use of their photographs.

JAN WILLIAMS and *PETER GOODING* who helped to find elusive photographs to complete the story.

MICHELLE CARRUTHERS who typed, typed and retyped.

BETTY SHANNON who cheerfully did everything she could to help me with the research at the Barbados Museum.

SHEILA WARD S.C.M. for her encouragement, especially in the early stages of writing, and for her loan of books, and knowledge of bygone Barbados.

EDWARD ELLIOT for always being there for me with practical help and encouragement.

WARREN ALLEYNE for his help and advice.

JOHN COLE whose keen interest and generosity was of enormous help and shows what a fine old Barbadian company Cole's Printery is.

RONALD WATSON a true professional who gave generously of his time, patience and professional expertise and was a joy to work with.

AUTHOR'S NOTE

My aim in this book is to share these old photographs and a piece of our past with other Barbadians and visitors to the island. In doing so, a small and simple piece of social history has emerged.

My own collection of photographs, made during my employment over many years in the rare stamp department of the philatelist, Stanley Gibbons, in London, together with pictures from the private collections of Dr. Karl Watson, Mr. Bill Ferguson and Mr. Peter Allard, form the nucleus of this book. We have used pictures from other sources, the ones which have been on loan to us have been listed in my acknowledgements.

The photographs illustrated in the book range from the earliest known photographs on the island, from 1860 up to roughly, the end of the First World War, and in a few cases a little later, to complete the story. To simplify matters further, I have attempted to make each page stand on its own with a description of the picture above; however if the book is read in its entirety, a brief history of the island will emerge.

I am sure that readers will wonder why some areas of life on the island have been omitted, and this is due entirely to the unavailability of photographs. Perhaps people will now come forward with photographs which may be included in another edition.

Many of the photographs speak for themselves, but I have described briefly the circumstances surrounding each picture and I share my recollections or understanding with the reader. Having a ninety-three year old father has been no small asset.

These photographs give us a wealth of information, they show a well ordered, law abiding church going and diligent island, with robust commerce, many gracious buildings, schools and churches, but it is the photographs of the true Barbadians which tell the story. There they are, of each race, showing the poverty and sheer hard grind of manual labour in the scorching sun. It shows the stamina and perseverance of our people; the standards of living of all the races and classes, intertwined or separate, are there for all to see.

For visitors, I hope that this book will help them to gain a further appreciation of the topography and history of this island, and help them to understand how we have arrived at where we are.

Ann Watson Yates
Barbados, 1998

MAP OF BARBADOS

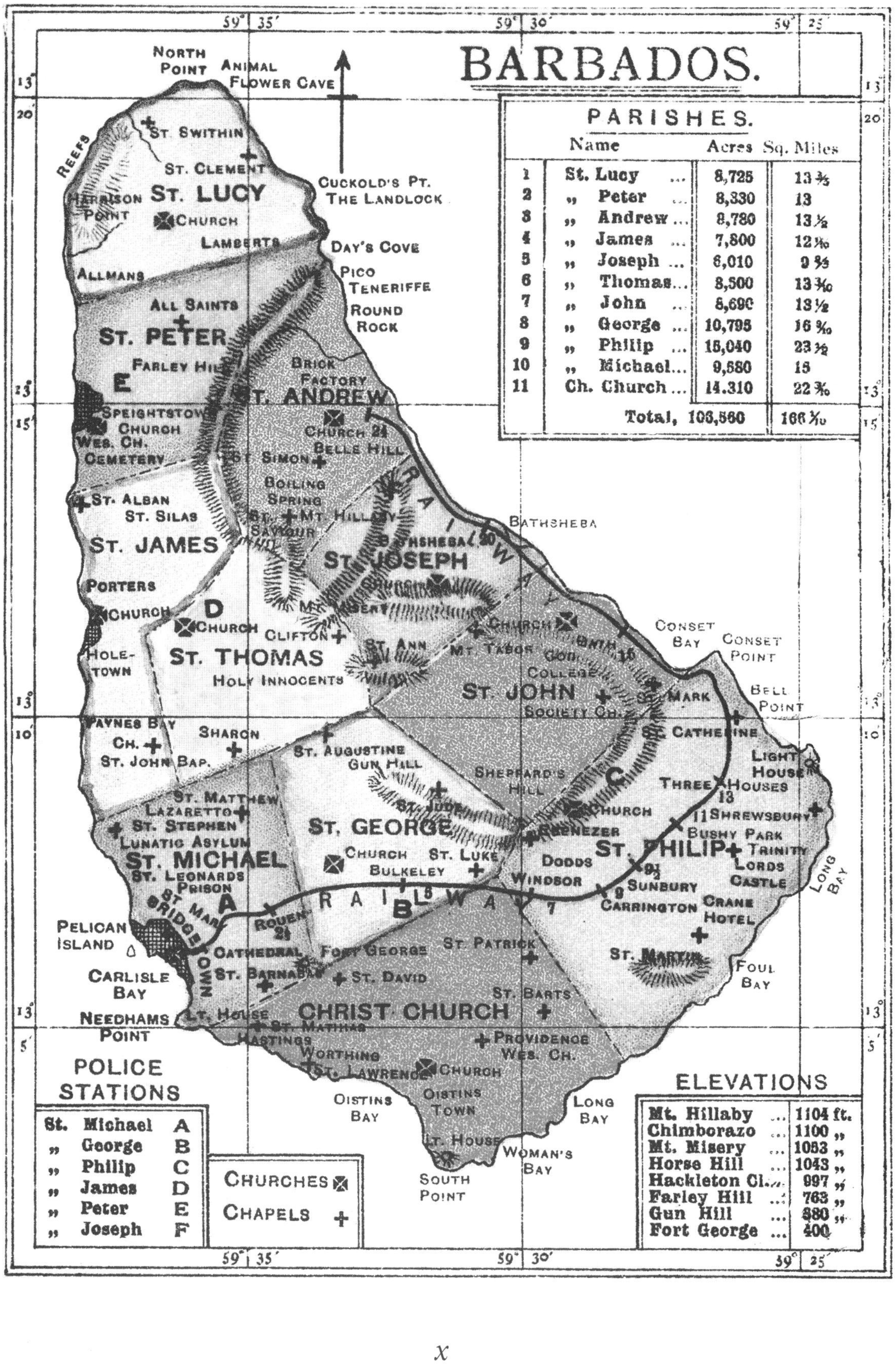

CONTENTS

LIST OF ILLUSTRATIONS

EARLY SETTLEMENT

BRIDGETOWN

THE RAILWAY

THE GARRISON

Map showing the location of Barbados

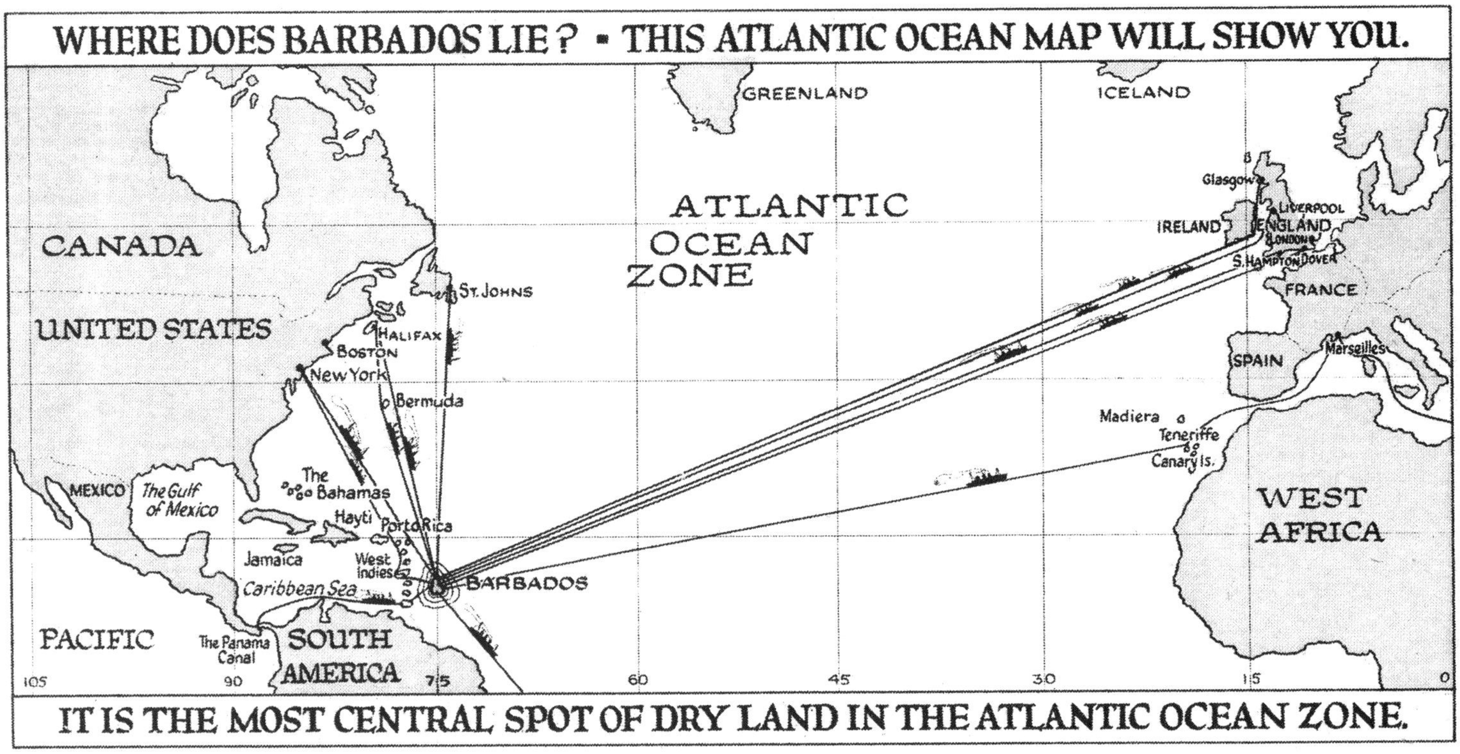

From an old Tourist Brochure circa 1900

Introduction

Photography was among the most significant discoveries of the nineteenth century. It was invented by scientists, but welcomed as an art form. It soon became an accepted method of recording a rapidly changing world – its people, cultures and landscapes. In addition, it has become a most useful form of documentation which has influenced us in complex ways. What is so valuable in an old photograph is the integrity of the camera in distinguishing the self-consciously artistic photograph from the "candid-camera" shots. The first practical photographic process was invented in Paris by M. Daguerre during the years 1824 to 1839. The light-sensitive plate was prepared by bringing iodine into contact with a plate of silver. After exposure, a positive image came by development of the plate in a mercury vapour. For open-air scenes, the first daguerreotypes involved exposures of five to ten minutes. The collodion process, first used in 1851, made this technique obsolete. In 1888 George Eastman's hand-held camera introduced the instancy of the snapshot. This revived the popularity of photography in a way that had not occurred since the mid-nineteenth century daguerreotype.

In Barbados, photography has been practised for approximately 150 years. The first advertisement by a photographer appeared in a newspaper called the *Barbados Globe* on 5th February, 1852. This photographer was a Mr J. Campion. By 1872, Mr W.G. Cooper had arrived from Scotland and opened a photographic studio in Bridgetown. There he introduced the glass plate negative process, melting down solid silver five-shilling pieces to obtain the nitrate of silver to make the light-sensitive solution.

From the inception of photography to the present day, photographers have rarely dated their photographs. One can only estimate the dates of old photographs by the length of the skirts, the growth of the trees, buildings, shop signs, gas lamps, trains, trams and tramlines (these appear only in Barbadian photographs from 1881–1926), and the presence or absence of motor vehicles. Another useful indication of approximate dates are the telephone wires which were carried on wooden frames or "horses" on rooftops between 1885 and 1910.

Photography has given us a vivid archive of a past way of life. The two best-known early photographers in Barbados were Mr W.G. Cooper and Mr H.W. Parkinson. We owe them a debt of gratitude for preserving for us bygone Barbados.

A Description of Barbados
(Major John Scott, 1667)

Barbados is the Crown and Font of all the Caribbee Islands towards the rising sun, being the most east of any, and lies more conveniently than any of the rest as a seat of war, being most healthful, fruitful and stored with all the things necessary of its innate growth which are necessary for life. The greatest mart for trade, not only of the Caribbees, but of any island in the West Indies, being inhabited with many wealthy planters and merchants, and hath very great conveniency for trade and in the time of war free from the danger of any enemy, except so powerful as to invade the island, which well managed would be too great a task for any Prince of Europe.

A reproduction of the Great Seal of Barbados made as a badge showing King Charles II as Neptune and King of Barbados

The Constitution of Barbados before Independence

Barbados was never a Crown Colony. It was the only colony in the British West Indies which retained the status known as the Old Representative System. This was a limited form of representative government founded on the Royal charter granted to Lord Carlisle in 1627. Before gaining independence in 1966, Barbados continued to possess a representative form of government. This gave the white freeholders all the liberties, franchises and privileges of the kingdom of England. It was known as Little England. The laws of the island were to be made with the consent of a majority of the free inhabitants (this would have excluded all women, Jews, free coloureds, slaves and indentured servants). The first House of Assembly met before 1640 and the policy which was founded was confirmed by the Charter of 1652 which ended a period of civil war on the island between royalist planters and parliamentary forces sent out by Cromwell's government. Articles of Agreement were signed which surrendered the island to the Commonwealth Government, which had replaced the monarchy in Great Britain with Oliver Cromwell.
The vital sections of the constitution, in substance, were:

No. 3: No taxes shall be levied on any of the inhabitants without their consent in a General Assembly.

No. 19: The government shall be by a governor, appointed by the Mother Country, a Council chosen by him, and an Assembly, chosen by a free and voluntary election of the freeholders of the island in the several parishes.

By the beginning of the twentieth century, the legislature consisted of three branches: the Governor, the Legislative Council, composed of nine nominated members, and the House of Assembly, composed of 24 elected members; two for each parish and two for the City of Bridgetown. The qualifications for appointment to the Legislative Council were ownership of freehold land worth £1,500 or an annual income of £200. The elective franchise was possessed by owners of land to the annual value of £5, occupiers of real property valued at £15, persons paying rates of £1 p.a. or earning £50 p.a. Doctors, lawyers, clergymen or any holder of a university degree were also eligible for election.

We still have little or no popular knowledge of our past though, granted, there is a serious disincentive to exploring that past: many people feel that there are only horror stories about slavery waiting back there for us, stories of the struggles of black Barbadians to get up out of the mud and eddoes and make something of their lives in a society dominated by a white European plantocracy on the one hand, and for a long time operated as a British garrison colony on the other.

*Kevyn Arthur (***Barbados Advocate** *newspaper, 1997)*

A medal struck to celebrate
the abolition of slavery in 1834

The solid foundation of our society is our love for, and our loyalty to, Barbados. Every Barbadian shares these feelings that transcend all political, religious, social, racial, age, gender and other differences. This strong foundation has served us well in the past, and will continue to serve and support us in our dealings with the challenges of the future.

*Sir John Stanley Goddard (***Barbados Advocate** *newspaper, 1997)*

A badge made for the
West Indian Produce Association.
The head was taken from an old Barbadian penny.

Amerindian Excavations at Chancery Lane

Amerindian Excavations at Chancery Lane

The Arawaks were the first inhabitants of Barbados. They came to the island in their dugout canoes from South America. These people had light skins, oriental eyes and straight hair; for the sake of simplicity they will be referred to as Amerindians.

Four distinct culture groups of these people occupied the island at different times; these facts are known through excavation sites and the analysis of various non-organic artifacts such as shell tools and shards of pottery, in fact anything which has not decomposed.

The first Amerindians to arrive were true stone-age, pre-ceramic people, who came about 2,000 years before the birth of Christ. The three other waves of migration saw the arrival of the Saladoid, the Troumassoid, and the Suazoid peoples. These three groups were able to make pottery, but oddly the pottery did not improve over time; the Saladoids made beautiful, finely decorated pottery, whereas the Suazoids' pottery was heavy and clumsy.

When the English settled in Barbados in 1627, their records indicate that they found no Amerindians on the island, possibly because the Spanish slave-raiding expeditions had driven them from the island. It is possible that a few may have remained behind or been visiting on a fishing expedition.

The earliest peoples who inhabited Barbados left no written records, except for the petroglyphs carved in the Springhead Cave in St James. They had approximately 50 known settlements, mostly along the coast; the three largest were at Bridgetown, Heywoods and Chancery Lane.

The Amerindians practised both deep-sea and reef fishing; they built fish traps, used vegetable poisons to stun fish and also used lines, nets and spears. They caught all sorts of fish, from sharks to flying fish, and ate shellfish and turtles. They also ate many species of birds, planted cassava as a staple in their diet and grew assorted squash, beans and peppers like other Indians in the Americas. They cultivated cotton for nets, fishing lines and rope, and they grew roucou for making red dye and body paint. Excavation of their graves shows that they believed in an after life, and it is entirely possible that they practised ritual cannibalism. The early settlers reported visits of Amerindians from St Vincent and St Lucia for magic or religious purposes (or perhaps they were simply hiding from an enemy); they would pull their canoes into the gullies and cover them with leaves. These visits ceased in the eighteenth century. The Arawak name for Barbados was Ichirouganaim.

BARBADIANS CIRCA 1880

Barbados, unlike its other English-speaking neighbours, has always had a large, poor white population. It averaged about 80% of the white population – so much for the myth that all of the white settlers were rich planters or merchants and slave owners.

In this picture, a poor white woman and a child sit outside their hovel under Chalky Mount, in the Scotland District; the hovel is thatched with dry cane trash. It is probable that this woman and child were the descendants of servants brought out from England by the early settlers, or freed indentured servants bought after settlement. One thing is certain, during indenture or slavery, accommodation on a plantation would have been superior to this hut, as many planters provided their labourers with stone-built huts after 1780.

The indentured labourers were people who sold or contracted themselves into slavery for three to seven years, or were people who had displeased the English government on religious or political grounds; they may also have been working off a large debt. They were usually sold for 1,550 pounds of sugar per man, and promises of clothing and land to be honoured at the end of their indenture. Needless to say, it was not in the interest of the planters for these people to survive their indentures, and their treatment was at times more brutal than that of the black slaves, who were more highly valued as they were physically stronger.

Scottish labourers were much favoured, and the seventeenth-century governor, Lord Willoughby, preferred them to the Irish who were considered troublemakers. The supporters of the Duke of Monmouth – who was defeated at Sedgemoor in 1685 when Protestants fought the rightful heir to the English throne, the Roman Catholic James I – were transported to work on the island. Later more arrived when Highlanders, taken prisoner at the battle of Culloden Moor in 1746, were exiled to work in the sugar cane fields of Barbados. They were often still wearing their kilts and their sunburnt legs gave rise to the derogatory term "Red Legs" which continues to be applied to this group.

BARBADIANS CIRCA 1890

In this posed photograph, two plantation labourers are captured in their workday clothes in front of a chattel house. The old man is wearing a tunic made from an old sugar bag (crocus bag), and on his head is a pad, often made of rags or plantain fibre. This indicates the loads this elderly man carried on his head daily.

The lady is better dressed because she was in charge of a child gang on a plantation. We know this because of the whip she carries. These were supposed to be kindly older women who "rarely used their whips". Her job would have been to ensure that the children did light weeding and other small agricultural jobs, but her main function was to keep them "out of mischief", and instil a work ethic. Some prominent white Barbadians today had great grandfathers who worked in child gangs, and like the others earned 11 cents a week.

These two people are the descendants of slaves, brought from the West African coast to work in the sugar cane fields. This disgraceful practice was taken up after the Spanish and Portuguese had virtually exterminated the island Amerindians who were even more physically unsuited to heavy labour than the European servants and labourers. Like the Red Legs, many Africans arrived as the hapless victims of local civil wars in their homeland, sold by their own chiefs to both Arabs and Europeans, or simply kidnapped and exchanged for ammunition, whisky or beads, as these commodities were needed. The hypocrites who bought these slaves on arrival (£30 for a man, £25 for a woman) were devout church goers and usually attended the Church of England every Sunday. This church supported the slave trade and the planters, from whom it derived financial support.

BARBADIANS CIRCA 1920

This is a mourning photograph taken of a family soon after the death of a planter, the owner of a plantation of 72 acres in St Thomas. In addition to his wife and himself, this planter supported four children by a wife who had died in childbirth, the seven in the photograph, an adopted niece, plus two destitute spinster sisters. They lived in a pretty plantation house, heavily mortgaged, and the planter made the initial annual repayments to his bank by the sale of bananas until he brought the plantation into order and his sugar cane was established; this he crushed in his own windmill and boiled the juice in his own boiling house. Before things could get any easier he died at the age of 46. The plantation was sold, the bank repaid, debts cleared and the family moved to Fontabelle where the older children left school and took jobs in Bridgetown. Not an uncommon story; at the time of this picture, sugar prices had started to crash after the boom during the First World War.

Who were the "plantocracy", and where did this word come from? Someone from "away" (overseas) I suspect. It may be a useful academic term used to indicate a governing class and/or a derogatory term, but very exaggerated for the majority of small plantation owners. It can only apply to a few Barbadian families ennobled by King Charles II for supporting the monarchy during the English Civil War and others who arrived on the island as titled people, or those whose titles were either bestowed for civic work, or often bought. The majority of down-to-earth Barbadians do not consider themselves part of the "plantocracy", nor would they wish to be considered as such; it is not the Barbadian style. As one local wit recently remarked, he had no desire to be a plutocrat, an aristocrat, or any other sort of rat!

The vast majority of plantations were very small, and unlike the other islands could not afford absentee landlords. The planters worked hard, lived off their land, and usually owed the bank money all their lives. Like all Barbadians of every colour and class, their strong bonds to family, and ties through marriage enabled them to survive.

Barbadians circa 1920

Here is a happy photograph of a wedding day. The entire wedding party is beautifully turned out, many of the clothes would have come from "away", probably America, and undoubtedly a lot of savings went into the celebration. All Barbadians love clothes, good food and drink, and entertaining. They observe the rites of passage through life in meticulous detail; their christenings, confirmations, weddings and funerals are sincerely and faultlessly performed. This wedding is not a society Bridgetown wedding of some doctor or lawyer; it is a middle class affair on which much time, energy and hard-earned money has been spent.

Barbadian love of hospitality is genuine and legendary, and this has always been so. Here is a description of a "breakfast" (lunch) party at the house of Mr and Mrs London Bourne in 1834. The party was given for two white visitors from the United States who had arrived on behalf of the American Anti-slavery Society (America abolished slavery 29 years after Barbados). London Bourne was born a slave and remained so until his father was able to buy his freedom at the age of 23. Despite all the discrimination of the time, he was able to work hard and make a considerable fortune. He owned several properties in Bridgetown and two plantations, Friendship and Grazettes, and was a highly respected member of the commercial community.

At the breakfast party, Mr and Mrs Bourne sat at either end of a large dining table, where Mrs Bourne presided with much dignity; Mr Bourne was affable with a sprightly intellect. In addition to the four, (two visiting Americans and two other guests) who sat to the right and left of the host and hostess, there was a son-in-law, an unmarried daughter, and an 11-year-old son about to leave for Edinburgh to finish his education. A generous Barbadian breakfast was served and the guests were very much taken with Mrs Bourne's dignity and grace. "Her occasional remarks were made with genuine modesty, and indicated good sense and discrimination." In spite of all this, London Bourne was refused membership of the Exchange, a Bridgetown merchants' club. It must have afforded him some satisfaction nevertheless to be the owner of the premises of this club!

A SEPHARDIC FAMILY PORTRAIT CIRCA 1880

A good history has yet to be written of the Sephardic Jews in Barbados. Expelled from the Iberian Peninsula at the end of the fifteenth century, they established communities in Protestant North Western Europe, especially in Amsterdam, Rotterdam and London. They were quick to seize the commercial opportunities offered by the Dutch invasion of the sugar producing area of Recife, Brazil (at the end of the sixteenth century). With the Portuguese reconquest and the reassertion of the Catholic Church, the Sephardic Jews were once again forced to flee, heading this time for the Caribbean, where they established footholds in Curacao, Suriname, St. Eustatius and Barbados, from where, subsequent migrations took them to Jamaica and the British North American Colonies.

Their role in the early economic development of Barbados is important, both as sources of capital, technological transfers for the infant Barbadian sugar industry, and their knowledge of and contacts in European markets.

This is a portrait of the Daniels family at their home Galba Lodge in Fontabelle, Bridgetown. Echoing a sad recurrent theme throughout this book, this property was demolished in 1998. The roots of this family in Barbados go back to the seventeenth century, through their D'Azevedo, Lindo, De Paz ancestors. Though the direct lines of these families have disappeared, they still have descendants in Barbados, from whom these family mementoes have come. Here we see Mr Daniels wearing a cork helmet, with his hand resting on his wife's shoulder, she was a Bonyun. They are accompanied by children, family friends and a trusted family retainer.

NANCY DANIELS

This photograph of Nancy Daniels is undoubtedly the oldest and most interesting picture in this book. Nancy looks serenely and confidently across the ages at us. Wearing a head tie and a fine brocaded dress and shawl, she sits, hands resting gently on a leather bound volume — the Bible, we think instinctively, but the gilt-edged title is too long — New Testament perhaps? The picture is posed, with a marble topped table on her right and a drawn, tasselled curtain to her left. In all probability, this was taken during the 1850's in a studio in Bridgetown, possibly by the photographer Campion who worked at this time. If not taken in a studio, then Nancy posed in the home of the Daniels family, for whom she worked for many years, first as a slave, and then a domestic servant.

Nancy was born in Africa, probably of Ibo ethnicity. We do not know her real name. Her entry in the volume housed at the Barbados Archives, records her death and burial on September 24, 1871 at St. Leonard's Church. Her age is officially given as 116 years. Little else is said about her, except that she was a domestic who resided at Synagogue Lane. Oral tradition in the Daniels Family from whom she took her surname, puts her age at 120 years. Accepting either version her year of birth would have been 1751 or 1755, making her possibly the longest lived person ever to have inhabited Barbados.

Her memories would have filled volumes. Her childhood in West Africa, capture, the Middle Passage, the Bridgetown Fire of 1766, the devastating hurricane of 1780, the 1816 slave revolt, Emancipation and Apprenticeship. Her life spanned fateful years, and her experiences are etched in her face.

BEARDED FIG TREES

In this photograph, some military gentlemen, probably from the Garrison, and a young girl with a donkey have made the trip to see the trees and record the event with a photograph.

It is said that because of the heavy growth of the aerial roots of these trees, Portuguese sailors referred to the island as "The Bearded Ones", which in Portuguese becomes "barbadas" or "barbados".

Barbados is noted on sixteenth-century maps as Barnados, San Bernardo and Barbudos; however it is generally accepted that a Portuguese sailor, on a voyage to Brazil, was among the first Europeans to visit the island, and that he gave the island the name of Las Barbadas. Tradition has it that he was one Pedro a Campos, and that it was his crew which put some "hogs" on the island to breed, with a view to the future needs of seamen. Certainly pigs were found by the early settlers.

The historian Froude was of the opinion that the name "Barbados" referred to a race of bearded Indians who inhabited the island.

The name of St Bernard, a Roman Catholic saint, was not likely to find favour with the Dutch and English Protestants and the Bearded Fig Tree legend was undoubtedly more acceptable to the settlers of that religion.

The Hole

In July 1625, a ship called the *Olive*, or the *Olive Blossom*, bound for Surinam in Dutch Guiana, was driven, through unskilful navigation, to the western shore of Barbados. The crew landed at or near where Holetown now stands. The *Olive Blossom* had been fitted out by Sir Olive Leigh, of Kent, with stores and settlers for his brother's plantation in Surinam. Captain Cataline and his crew, finding the island unoccupied, took possession of it in the name of James I of England; they erected a wooden cross and carved "James K of E and of this island". A fustic tree, with some of the names of the first settlers, is alleged to have stood until destroyed in the hurricane of 1780.

In February 1627, the *William and John*, a vessel of 100 tons fitted out by Sir William Courteen, a wealthy Dutch merchant who had the patronage of the future Earl of Pembroke, and commanded by Captain Henry Powell, approached Barbados. On board were 40 white, male settlers, and eight black men whom they had taken on board in the Atlantic as Portuguese booty. After sailing around the island, the *William and John* anchored in "The Hole", near where the *Olive Blossom* had anchored two years earlier to claim the island for England. The first settler to step ashore was one William Arnold. The settlers erected a fort, named it "Plantation Fort", hoisted the English flag, and elected Captain William Deane to be in charge.

Englishmen knew about Barbados before 1625; their knowledge would have been derived from reports from Spanish and Portuguese ships' captains who periodically visited the island from the beginning of the sixteenth century. Richard Hakluyt, Archdeacon of Westminster, mentions it in the third and last volume of his book: *The Principal Navigations, Voyages, Traffics, and Discoveries of the English Nation.* This book was published in 1600.

The Holetown Monument

The Holetown Monument was erected in 1905 near to the Hole in St James to celebrate the claiming of Barbados by the English. Owing to a miscalculation over the date, the tercentenary celebrations should have taken place 20 years later than they did.

Immediately after landing the party in February 1627, Captain Powell of the *William and John* sailed to Essequibo in Guiana, where he obtained from an old Dutch comrade named Groenewegel, seeds, roots and plants. Among the food crops he brought from Guiana were cassava, yams, indian corn, sweet potatoes, plantains, bananas and oranges, limes, pineapples, sugar cane, tobacco, cotton and the anatto plant which produces a red dye. He also thoughtfully brought some Amerindian families to teach the colonists how to grow these crops. Although Barbados was richly wooded, there were few natural crop species, the island having been deserted so long.

Soon after Captain Powell's return from Guiana, his brother John arrived on *The Peter* with 50 more Englishmen. Captain John Powell was elected the first governor. For years the early settlers lived in small wooden huts and often had to plant their crops between the branches of the trees they had felled. In addition to the crops brought from Guiana, their diet consisted of the pigs left on the island by the Portuguese to breed, along with the plentiful supply of fish. It is doubtful if the Amerindian families were ever taken back to Guiana with the agricultural tools they had been promised.

THE CONSTITUTION RIVER

On the 5th July 1628, 64 more settlers arrived at the swampy and unhealthy mouth of a small "river". A primitive Indian bridge spanned this malodorous stream, and the area faced a wide bay. The owner of this land was the Earl of Carlisle; unable to pay his debts in England, he was forced to give 10,000 acres of land in Barbados to merchants in England in settlement of his debts. The merchants formed a syndicate, called the Rawdon Syndicate, after Sir Marmaduke Rawdon. It was this syndicate which sent out the second wave of early settlers. Each settler was given a grant of 100 acres of land, and a further 100 acres were set aside for general use.

The 10,000 acres given to the early settlers extended from Bridgetown up the St George Valley, which has the richest soil on the island. Houses and storehouses sprang up in a haphazard way. This settlement became Bridgetown, the bay was named Carlisle Bay and the Indian river became known as the Constitution River. This small river which drains the parishes of St Michael and St George, is also an arm of the tidal area of the sea. In early Bridgetown it was deep enough for sloops to sail about a mile inland. Mangroves grew in its foul-smelling swamp, which was also reported to be crawling with crabs. So now there were two groups of settlers on the island: the first group in Holetown under the patronage of the future Earl of Pembroke, and the new settlers in Bridgetown and up the St George Valley under the patronage of the Earl of Carlisle. The scene was set for trouble.

Carlisle Bay

Barbados is deficient in good natural harbours, Carlisle Bay being an open roadstead, or piece of water near shore at which ships can ride at anchor. In spite of this, most of the famous British Admirals anchored in Carlisle Bay: Rodney, Jervis, Collingwood and Nelson, to name the more distinguished. For small craft, the inner harbour or careenage, protected by the "Molehead", afforded a safe anchorage. The advantage of Carlisle Bay was that it was easy for large ships to come and go at night; there was no risk of entering through a narrow passage, and there was no delay or trouble in turning around as there would have been in a small land-locked harbour.

In the last quarter of the previous century, not more than three days in any year were ever lost through rough seas preventing the unloading and loading of ships in Carlisle Bay. Pictorial evidence over the centuries shows the busy nature of this Bay, as sometimes entire fleets anchored in the roadstead. Barbados became a major transhipment port and the hub of the eastern Caribbean. Certainly in the seventeenth and eighteenth centuries, along with London and Boston, it formed a triangle that anchored the British Mercantile system in the North Atlantic.

THE PIERHEAD
(FORMERLY KNOWN AS THE MOLEHEAD)

The men in the foreground of this picture are working with coal for the ships. In 1770, to raise money for the construction of the pier and wharf, a tonnage duty was imposed on shipping, and towards this goal the British government also made a grant of £5,000. The pier in this picture was the one which was rebuilt after the hurricane of 1831. The supervision of the building of this pier was the responsibility of the Royal Engineers who were quartered at the Garrison. Construction began in 1837 and was completed by 1846.

THE BUSY CAREENAGE

In this picture the Careenage is full of schooners used for the inter-island trade. In the foreground lightermen row their heavy lighters(a misnomer if ever there was one) to bring cargo out of the ships in Carlisle Bay and to ferry out Barbadian cargo.

These flat bottom boats were built of very thick planks and were of two sizes, some of 20 and others of 30 tons laden. They took great strength and skill to manoeuvre.

The Wharf

Even in the days of private landing places, in the seventeenth and early eighteenth centuries, a part of the Bridgetown waterfront was set aside as a public wharf. Because the channel frequently became impassable, due to wrecks, silt and the habit of throwing Bridgetown's rubbish into the Careenage, dredging was necessary from time to time and it was decided that a public wharf and pier should be constructed. It became necessary that vessels drawing up to ten feet of water should be able to go up channel, if required, for careening and repair, as well as for the unloading of smaller cargoes.

The wharf in Bridgetown was always very busy, the out-going smell of molasses and sugar always in the air, mingled with the in-coming smell of saltfish, pigtails and onions past their prime.

CAREENING

The Careenage was formed by the lower reaches of the Constitution River. The name comes from the word "careen" which means to turn a ship onto her side for repairs. This was done by attaching weights to the mast and pulling the ship over; once on her side the ship was cleaned of moss and barnacles. If it had been sailing to British Guiana or some other similar areas, its wooden bottom would also be infested by a worm the size of a man's forefinger and with a head like an auger; these worms were known as Toredos and would have to be removed.

Once cleaned on one side, the ship would be turned onto her other side by the same method and the process repeated. This facility was available to the large number of ocean-going ships and inter-island schooners which came into Carlisle Bay. All other dry dock facilities were also available.

The Dry Dock

Barbados could boast a fine dry dock and first-class workmanship in that dock. The port was very busy and used by several steamship companies: the Royal Mail Steamers from Southampton, Scruttons Steamships from London, the East Asiatic Line, and the Leyland and Harrison Lines from Liverpool. Steam ships trading between the United States and Brazil called at Barbados, the Booth Steamship Co., Hamburg South American Line, Lloyd Brazileiro Line, Lamport and Holt and the Quebec line, to name a few.

The dry dock's screw-lifting dock was 240 feet long by 46 feet wide, capable of lifting 1,200 tons dead weight, and could take on vessels drawing not more than 14 feet of water.There were three foundries in 1915 capable of undertaking repairs to ship machinery. The shipwright work was excellent, materials for carrying out this work could be obtained in bond, and a good supply of all necessary stock was always kept on hand.

In addition to all this, fresh provisions were cheap and plentiful; the water was of excellent quality and was supplied by two steam water boats at the price of one shilling five and a half pence per 100 gallons.

PUNCHEONS ON THE WHARF 1907

This photograph shows casks or barrels for sugar, molasses or rum, waiting for shipment, and the hive of activity in Bridgetown, especially on the wharf.

Hogsheads and puncheons were 100-140 gallons and barrels were half that size. All these were made by coopers, and most of the large plantations had their own coopers. There were cooperage yards in and around Bridgetown where the smaller plantations could buy puncheons.

These casks were made of imported wood, and bound with metal bands. As they weighed 600 pounds each, rolling them was a lot easier than lifting them. In the busy streets of Bridgetown, they were placed on a flimsy looking two-wheeled cart called a "spider". It took two men to pull a spider and one, with some skill, to navigate.

A SCHOONER LEAVING THE CAREENAGE

Many Barbadians owned schooners and traded between the islands and the South American coast. They mostly carried ground provisions and hogs and brought back fine woods, citrus fruit and sometimes gold from British Guiana. This form of commerce was one of the ways that men of no private means made the minimum deposit on a plantation. Other Barbadian families to this day have sailing in their blood from generations in this trade.

Construction of the West Wing of the Public Buildings circa 1870

In 1860 there was a great fire in this area of Bridgetown, which started in the lumber yard of the Alleyne brothers. Having destroyed a large area to the south and then the upper wharf, the fire jumped the Careenage and consumed the entire area on either side of lower Bay Street, up to Shurlands Alley. Many houses and shops which clustered around the Square were burnt. The Square was much smaller in those days, and the fire enabled the government to lay out plans for the area in a way that had not been possible before.

The land was purchased by the government and six architects submitted plans to the Public Buildings Erection Committee. These buildings were erected from the designs of Mr J T Bourne, Superintendent of Public Works. The estimated cost was £15,530. Four tenders were presented to the Committee by local builders, and the lowest one accepted. The corner stone was laid on 16th June, 1870. The building was completed by the end of 1871 at a cost of £13,750, and handed over to the government in 1872.

THE CHAMBERLAIN SWING BRIDGE CIRCA 1905

In this picture of the bridge, Barbadians are enjoying a bank holiday to celebrate the tercentenary anniversary of the claiming of Barbados for King James I. In their enthusiasm, they celebrated 20 years too early due to misinformation widely circulated regarding the date of settlement.

The redevelopment of the Trafalgar Square area included an inner basin capable of receiving ships of a fairly large size. It was decided that the West Bridge spanning the Careenage be replaced by a swing bridge. Construction began in 1865, but unfortunately the builder took it upon himself to change the original plans, and what he finally erected caused so much disagreement that it had to be dismantled. The ironwork for the bridge had been ordered from London; when it arrived in pieces and was assembled, the two sides did not meet. One side had to be replaced by a concrete structure that could not swing. The bridge finally cost £17,909 19s 10d; probably the most expensive monument to mismanagement and waste of public funds in Barbados in its time. It was named after Mr Joseph Chamberlain, the British prime minister, whose government had voted a generous grant of money to the island for the building of the bridge. This bridge has since been renamed the Independence Bridge.

The Statue of Admiral Horatio Nelson, Upper Broad Street

In this picture the celebratory arches around Lord Nelson bear his last words, "Thank God I Have Done My Duty". On 20th December 1805, the news reached Barbados of Admiral Nelson's great victory off Cape Trafalgar on the southern coast of Spain. This distinguished British admiral had spent much of his career in the West Indies and visited Barbados many times. Apparently he did not like Barbados very much. The last time that Admiral Nelson was to anchor in Carlisle Bay was 4th June 1805; looking for the enemy, he sailed to Trinidad, and then chased after them across the Atlantic. On 21st October, the battle was fought off Cape Trafalgar, the British under Nelson, and the combined French and Spanish fleets under Villeneuve and Gravina respectively. It was a complete victory for the British, but their admiral was one of the many killed. This victory ensured British naval supremacy during the rest of the Napoleonic Wars, which was crucial for the trade between Britain and her colonies on the other side of the Atlantic; in fact, it was their lifeblood. Barbadians for their part were grateful and relieved not to become a French West Indian Colony, which was the alternative.

On Sunday 5th January 1806, a memorial service was held in St Michael's Parish Church, now the Cathedral. Within days a subscription list was opened to raise funds for a memorial statue; by 25th February, £2,324 2s 6d had been subscribed by people from all walks of life. The statue was cast in bronze by Sir Richard Westmacott in England, and erected on 22nd March 1813, with great pomp and ceremony. Years later, in the 1840s, the British began to erect their own monument to Nelson in London's Trafalgar Square.

LOWER BROAD STREET CIRCA 1872

This photograph of Lower Broad Street shows one of the earliest photographic studios on the island. It was in this studio that Mr Cooper introduced the glass plate negative process, melting down solid silver five-shilling pieces to obtain the nitrate of silver to make the light-sensitive solution.

It is not clear when the rather exaggerated name of Broad Street was first used for this narrow road. Over the years it has had many other names. The Statute of 1657 declared it reserved as a market place and for other public purposes of the island. It was given the name of Cheapside; now only its western extension, the area near St Mary's Church, retains this name. Later in the 17th century it was called the Exchange Street, because the Merchants Exchange was situated there. One other name was New England Street. It has probably been called Broad Street since about 1703. Travellers' accounts record that it has always been the premier street of Bridgetown, used by the mercantile elite of the day. It was invariably described as being lined with elegant, well-stocked shops, which could satisfy the most discriminating of shoppers. The French Jesuit priest Labat who visited the island in 1700 was particularly generous in his praise of the buildings and shops of Broad Street.

Swan Street

The larger streets of early Bridgetown were reputedly laid out by John Swann, one of Governor Wolverstone's captains who was also a surveyor. According to tradition, Swan Street was named after him. To confuse the issue, there was also a tavern there called "The Swan", so for one or both of these reasons Swan Street was given its name. Most of the early Sephardic Jewish population lived in Swan Street over their stores, and the street was often referred to as "Jew's Street". The street was characterised by overhanging balconies, from which in the cool of the evening families would engage their neighbours in conversation, or listen to the repartee in the street below.

ROEBUCK STREET

Roebuck Street began as a track in 1653. There was a gully at its upper end, and at this time a bridge was built over the gully which was known as the Causeway. A popular tavern called "The Roebuck" was built there by Thomas Noell, a former London merchant, and undoubtedly related to Martin Noell, the well-known trader in indentured labourers. Between 1672 and 1679, "The Roebuck" was the favourite meeting place of the Barbados Council as well as the General Assembly.

In the nineteenth century, Roebuck Street became the focus of the provision trade and, as this photograph illustrates, became a hive of activity, marked by a constant flow of mule-drawn carts, or heavily laden two wheeled push carts or "spiders" drawn by men.

The Brigade Station No. 2 with Hand-Drawn Cart

In 1913 there were six fire stations and the fire brigade numbered 25 men. The Central Fire Brigade Station was in Bridgetown and it was linked to the district stations by telephone. The Barbados Telephone Company was started in 1882, and was operational in 1883, less than ten years after Alexander Graham Bell's first telephone in 1873. By 1886 important public utilities and businesses had telephone numbers (just two digits).

In this photograph are five firemen with their hand-drawn cart which was pulled by a rope on each side. There is a coil of hose between the rear wheels, several buckets on the cart itself, and a large axe above the buckets. The box at the back would have contained a first-aid kit and other small items. The photograph was taken by Mr A.E. Shannon whose studio was at 4 High Street, Bridgetown.

Street Watering, Corner of James Street circa 1880

This was done for health reasons. Roads were not tarred in those days, and few paved with stones. The white dust stirred up by the horse-drawn traffic, in particular, was considered very unhealthy and a contribution to the transmission of disease. The streets were watered each morning following a noisy garbage collection by mule cart at 4.00 am. In 1753, a visitor to the island, Dr Robert Poole, commented in his journal, "the streets are subject here to be extremely dusty, especially those parts that are not paved". Barbadians are to this day very aware of hygiene and even in poverty strive to obtain a high standard.

This early photograph is of some significance. The most prominent building on the left is regarded as the oldest structure in Bridgetown, built in the Dutch fashion, probably in the 1660s. In this photograph the building appears to retain its pantile roofing, though in recent years this has been replaced. The other building has a fine wrought-iron balcony and a lookout tower from which clerks would scan the horizon for incoming shipping, thus providing valuable mercantile information for their employers.

THE SYNAGOGUE CIRCA 1908

Synagogue Nidhe Israel (Scattered of Israel) represents the coming and going of Barbadian Jewry since early settlement.

As early as 1628, one Abraham Jacobs was writing to the Earl of Carlisle from Barbados. The synagogue and cemetery on Synagogue Lane were established in 1654 and public worship allowed that year, three years ahead of London. That building was destroyed by the hurricane of 1831 and the present synagogue, depicted in this photograph was rebuilt on the old foundations. It was opened in March 1833 with an impressive ceremony, which was attended by the social elite of the island.

The major Jewish settlement in Barbados was founded in 1654 as a direct consequence of the Spanish Inquisition. Expelled from Spain during the reign of Ferdinand and Isabella, Jews moved to Portugal. During the short time that Spain and Portugal became one kingdom, they were forced to move on again. From Lisbon they immigrated to Amsterdam and then to Recife in Brazil, which was under Dutch domination at that time. They lived there peacefully until 1654 when Recife was reclaimed by the Portuguese. Many returned to Amsterdam where the Lord Protector of England, Oliver Cromwell, was petitioned by them to be allowed to settle in Barbados. This usually intolerant Puritan agreed and, amazingly, they were given "…the privileges of laws and statutes relating to foreigners and strangers". This, of course, would not have included the right to vote.

By 1926 Mr Edmund Baeza was the only practising Jew on the island; the others had left or converted to Anglicanism. The beautiful interior fittings were stripped out of the synagogue, which became the offices of the Barbados Turf Club.

The Montefiore Fountain, Lower Broad Street

The eastern end of Broad Street was known as the Green and the western end as the Lower Green. In this picture is the Montefiore Fountain situated in the Lower Green, given by the Jewish businessman John Montefiore in memory of his father in 1864. The fountain is made in the Neo-Gothic decorative style, and the gift of the fountain would have been quite in keeping with contemporary stories of the Jewish community at that time in Barbados; they are recorded as being charitable and pious, and a model of the sanctity of family life.

These Sephardic Jews were mostly merchants. Some had ships for trading, but the most important contribution they made to the island was the fact that having come from Brazil, they had the knowledge of the culture of sugar cane and sugar manufacturing. They were able to give the Barbadian planters valuable help and instruction as they fought to establish sugar on the island. In the Jewish cemetery, names like Massiah, Lindo, Da Costa, Gomes, Mordecai, Henriques and Montefiore are all recorded, and are now well-known names throughout the West Indies.

It took the Second World War and the Holocaust to send the second wave of Jews to Barbados. Mr Kreindler, Mr Altman, and other Ashkinazi Jews from northern Europe, have been a great asset to the island. The Montefiore Fountain was moved close to the synagogue, which has been restored in every detail as befits one of the oldest synagogues in the Western Hemisphere.

THE TRAFALGAR SQUARE AREA

This picture helps us to see the many changes which have taken place in Trafalgar Square over the years. The schooners have now sailed away from the Careenage for the last time, Admiral Nelson faces the opposite direction, the buggies have been replaced by cars, the tramlines have been ripped up, and the evergreen tree cut down.

One is struck by the elegant dress of the people in this photograph, in contrast to the tourists of today. All Barbadians still dress up to go into Bridgetown and would not dream of wearing beach attire when visiting the city.

A Fine Little Capital: the Public Buildings, Bridgetown circa 1880

In this lovely view of the Public Buildings from across the Careenage, Bridgetown is as fine a little capital as one could find anywhere. The stones in the foreground are ballast from the ships which arrived partially full of merchandise and returned fully laden with syrup, molasses, sugar and rum.

To the left is the Chamberlain Swing Bridge which could not quite swing completely. To the right is the east wing of the Public Buildings with its original large clock tower. This tower began to crack and sink within ten years of its construction and had to be demolished, redesigned and rebuilt. During this time of rebuilding the clock itself was put into safe keeping in a cell at Glendairy Prison to prevent pilfering. The redesigned clock tower with the reassembled clock was shifted to the west wing in 1880 and has remained in this position since that date.

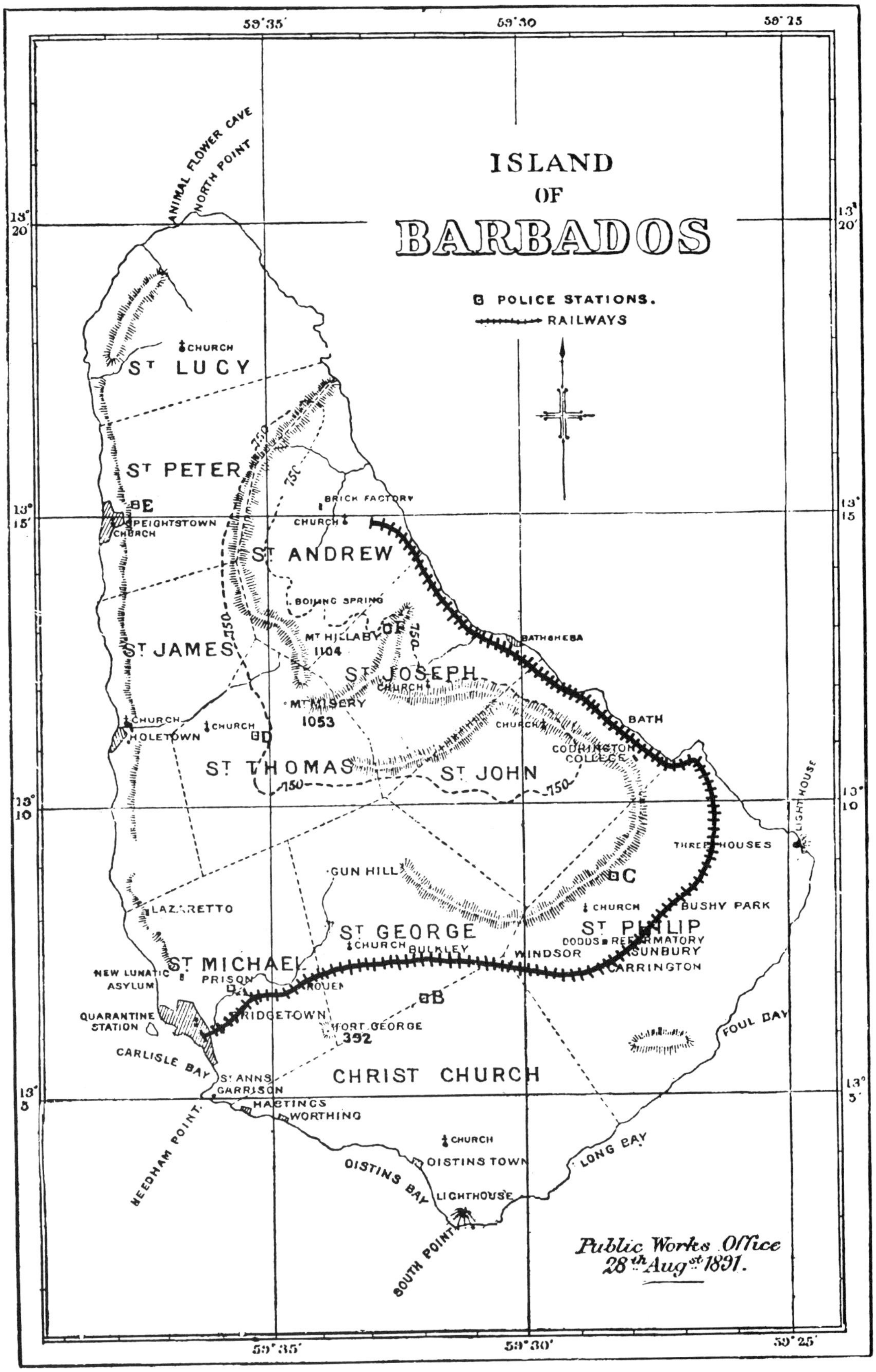

Railway map: Island of Barbados (1891)

A View of Bridgetown from the Railway Station

By 1874, Bridgetown looked much as it does in this picture. Starting from the left-hand side of the photograph are stacked imported pipes. Above this at the top of Broad Street and behind the evergreen tree is the site of the former infamous Bridgetown Cage. This cage was used by the Provost Marshal for the detention of minor offenders of both races and sexes. Rioting seamen, runaway slaves, drunks, thieves and whores were put into what became a permanent penal institution in the heart of Bridgetown.

Piped water had been introduced to Bridgetown in 1861, and the fountain was built and water flowing in it by 1865. The fountain was inaugurated in the presence of a large crowd, a guard of honour, an artillery salute, and the chiming bells of St Michael's Cathedral. Everyone wore their best clothes.

Trafalgar Square had been enlarged, and the statue of Nelson, had been erected surrounded by iron rails. The Swing Bridge had opened, as had the West Wing of the Public Buildings. The East Wing is seen with the original huge clock tower. Stacked wood for the lumber yards can be seen on the right forefront of the picture.

The Bridgetown Railway Terminus

The only way to Bathsheba with heavy luggage was by train; prior to that it was a hazardous journey by horse or mule. The Barbados Railway was actually five successive companies:

The Barbados General Railway	1846–1850
The Barbados Railway Company	1881–1898
The Bridgetown and St Andrew's Railway Ltd	1898–1905
The Barbados Light Railway Company Ltd	1905–1905
The Barbados Government Railway	1906–1937

Mr E.A. Stoute, a local historian, remarked that Barbadians used to joke that the railway was mentioned in the Bible as being "one of the creeping things that crawl on the face of the earth".

At one spot with a severe gradient, students from the nearby theological college sometimes had to come out to push the train. The Railway Rule Book was also basic: "If the engine be defective, the sooner the train can be stopped the better."

It was a rule of thumb that, in times of difficulty, the third-class passengers got out and pushed, while the second-class passengers got out and walked alongside, and the first-class passengers remained seated, no doubt offering verbal solace to the lesser-ranked passengers.

Train Crossing a Bridge circa 1882

From its inception, the railway was dogged by financial problems. This was the reason for the government's eventual closure of the railway in 1937.

The Barbados General Railway was supposed to run from Bridgetown to Speightstown. Unfortunately, the company collapsed before construction even started, due to lack of funds.

In 1878 a Mr Robert Fairlie visited the island and submitted a report for a new railway system, this time to be called the Barbados Railway Company. Once again it was supposed to reach Speightstown, but it never did. Instead of running straight up the west coast, it ran east from Bridgetown and terminated at Belleplaine. The first part of the line finally opened between Bridgetown and Carrington, St Philip in 1881, and the section to Belleplaine was completed in August, 1883.

The line was lightly built, with light rails, sharp curves and steep gradients; all the rolling stock was four-wheeled, with high axle loading; the gauge of the railway line was 3 feet 6 inches; and the engines used coal to make the steam.

Unfortunately, the contractor, finding costs greater than anticipated, cut more and more corners in the construction, and made ever-steeper gradients to reduce the cost of the earth works.

The Consett Cutting 1883

This picture of the Consett Cutting was taken soon after its completion in August 1883. The Cutting was also known as "My Lady's Hole". The train had to ascend a gradient of one in 31, which was steeper than the steepest railway gradient in England, and said by some to be the steepest in the world (without benefit of rack and pinion).

Going through the cutting had always been considered one of the thrills of the trip. However a tragedy occurred when three young boys stole a ride on one of the open cane cars. At the Consett Cutting the last three cars became unhooked and rolled back down the hill at an ever-increasing speed. One boy managed to jump off, while another held on and was badly injured by being scraped along the cutting; the third boy who had held on the longest jumped to his death on the coastal side of the track where he was impaled on some metal track which had been driven into the ground in an attempt to halt erosion.

The three cars continued to career along for well over a mile past Bath Station before they stopped by College Savannah.

A Full Train at Tent Bay

In this picture, two planters in white drill suits and cork hats watch the approaching train, always considered to be something of an event.

The trip from Bridgetown to Belleplaine was 23 miles and took two hours. There were three classes of seats, later reduced to first and third. The train left Bridgetown daily at 4:30 pm, except on Sundays when it departed at 7:40 am. On Wednesdays there was an extra train, so a round trip was possible on Sundays and Wednesdays. The first-class journey one way cost 60¢ and third-class 24¢. Mr Blenman was the ticket collector.

When the train left Bridgetown, the first stop was at Rouen, two-and-a-half miles away, then came stops at Bulkeley, Windsor, Carrington, Sunbury and Bushy Park. Here, in the early days, passengers would leave the train for the Crane Hotel, having made prior arrangements with the hotel-keeper to be met at the station by a carriage; the branch line from Carrington to the Crane was added in 1905. After leaving Bushy Park, the train continued to Three Houses, Bath, Bathsheba and terminated at Belleplaine.

In this picture, a full train makes its way past Tent Bay as it approaches Bathsheba Station. The train had American-styled passenger cars and there was always a festive atmosphere on the train, with complete strangers chatting during the journey, and often sharing food during breakdowns.

A Train Approaching Bathsheba Station

In this picture, a train from Bridgetown is about to pull in to Bathsheba Station. In the background on top of the hill is the outline of the Beachmount Hotel, a popular honeymoon hotel in its day.

By 1896, the Barbados Railway Company was becoming untenable and a petition was placed before the House of Assembly calling for its voluntary conclusion. This attempt was rejected by the House, but further borrowing was refused by the banks. The railway line running close to the beach suffered continuous erosion and corrosion, bad weather had destroyed whole sections of line along the coast and virtually no repairs or replacements had taken place during the seventeen years of the Barbados Railway Company. Budgets, such as they were, had never taken into account the rapid deterioration of metal in the seaspray on the east coast; also the lines at Three Houses required complete replacement because trains had to back up a good distance then run through the plantation at speed in order to climb the bank.

The Railway Company bond holders decided to bring over an engineer, a Mr Everard Calthrop, of the Barsi Light Railway in India, to assess the railway's future. Mr Calthrop was startled to discover that almost every basic principle of railway construction had been violated in Barbados to a most serious degree. The 3 feet 6 inch gauge was too wide for the sharp curves, axle loads too much for the weight of the rail, and the worn out locomotives would have to be discarded.

The Barbados Railway Company went into voluntary liquidation and was sold in Chancery in 1898 to bond holders of a new company called "The Bridgetown and St Andrew's Railway Limited".

TRAIN CROSSING THE BRIDGE OVER LONG POND

The three biggest bridges which the train had to cross were those over the Constitution River, Joe's River and Long Pond. The three major thrills of the trip to Belleplaine were reckoned to be the Joe's River and Long Pond Bridges, the other being the Consett Cutting.

When the construction of the Bridgetown and St Andrew's Railway started, the rail gauge was reduced to 2 feet 6 inches on Mr Calthrop's recommendation, and the new locomotives were bought from Baldwin and Co. in Philadelphia. The Number I engine was called "Alice", the Number II "Beatrice" and the Number III "Catherine". There were a total of five engines, four replacing three, etc.

There was a curtailed service in 1898, but normal service resumed in 1899. The original railway had enjoyed a government subsidy of £6,000 p.a. This new company lost that subsidy and operated at a loss each year until its liquidation in April 1905. Another new group which called themselves the "Barbados Light Railway Co. Ltd" was then formed.

The Return Journey from Belleplaine to Bridgetown

Holiday-makers, local people, a planter and a policeman watch the train approaching the Bathsheba Station on its way back to Bridgetown.

The Barbados Light Railway initiated an ambitious schedule, but by October, 1906 the Company was complaining of small passenger loads. This new Company earned £1,762 from passengers, £3,243 from freight, and the government grant was renewed at £2,000 p.a.

This was enough to cover expenditure. By the outbreak of the First World War, maintenance costs were rising and repairs being postponed. The government decided to cut the subsidy at this time, and yet another railway company went into liquidation. Late in 1915, the government finally took control and renamed the service "The Barbados Government Railway".

BATHSHEBA STATION: THE RETURN JOURNEY

The train from Belleplaine comes steaming into Bathsheba Station; its sign is shown clearly on the right of the picture. Goods and passengers wait on the platform to board the train. To the right of the station, wooden pallets are stacked to assist in the moving of goods. To the left of the station and behind the engine is a disused carriage which had been put on piles to be used as a public rest room.

The "Barbados Government Railway" imported a beautiful carriage engine to run as a single unit along the line; it was to be used particularly for excursion purposes. This engine came with Westinghouse air brakes, but as no one knew how to use them legend has it that they were immediately disconnected and replaced by manual brakes. This accomplished, the expensive new carriage engine was taken on a run down to Bathsheba. Unfortunately, it was unable to climb the steep incline and an ordinary engine had to be brought down to pull it out of Bath because it could not make the Consett gradient. After this trial run it was never used again, as it was seen as unfit for the journey.

TRAINSPOTTING

Children sit on the sleepers of the railway line. They were in no danger, as trains could be seen coming from a great distance; in addition, the driver was keen to use his whistle whenever possible.

During the 1920s, inadequate maintenance standards continued. The consulting engineers Law and Connell documented the mismanagement of resources, unsafe bridges, a depleting stock of spares, improper use or lack of use of brakes on the locomotives. In Bridgetown on a few occasions, the brakes failed completely and the train burst through the Triangle and started to go down the wharf. This problem was soon solved by removing some of the track, heating the remaining lines and turning them up in the air to a height of approximately two feet. When the brakes failed, this acted as a buffer of sorts.

THE DESERTED RAILWAY LINE 1937

In January, 1934, Mr Connell, the consulting engineer, stopped a tourist special leaving Bridgetown because the Belle Gully Bridge was unsafe. The passenger service never ran again. Soon after this, the bridge over Long Pond collapsed and the goods service from Bridgetown had to terminate at Bathsheba.

This restricted goods service continued but, when another report estimated a cost of £41,000 for rehabilitation, the government had to decide between spending money on extensive public roads or on the railway. It was decided to abandon the railway.

One of its main objectives had been to serve the sugar industry, but it was only ever utilised by nine of the 29 major sugar factories. In the meantime the taxpayers themselves were neglected after the closure of the passenger service and the concentration on freight. The east coast however, had been opened up by the railway line to the possibility of tourism and holiday-makers.

The railway finally closed in 1937 as lorries and a public road system brought to an end its chaotic history. The rolling stock was sold off and the lines pulled up and sold as scrap. Some of the former railway bridges are identifiable as road bridges, and in places it is possible to recognise the route of the railway line. After the disbandment of the railway, one of the drivers named Washi King worked at the Guinea Plantation, where his colleagues frequently asked him to "blow his whistle", which he always did obligingly. For those who can remember, it remains a romantic memory of their youth.

ST ANN'S CASTLE, THE GARRISON CIRCA 1913

This picture is of St Ann's Castle (or Fort) which was started in 1709. Along with Charles Fort and Beckwith Battery, it was built to protect Bridgetown and defend the island. The very earliest Fort at the Garrison area was built 23 years after settlement, as the early settlers took responsibility for their own defence. It was known as Needhams Fort, and was built of saplings and branches. Subsequently rebuilt using massive blocks cut from the coral cap of the island, it mounted 36 cannons, and was described in the diary of Major George Washington, the first President of the United States of America. He dined there four times with his consumptive brother Lawrence as the guests of Captain Petrie, the Officer-in-Command.

St Ann's Fort was built as a separate unit 700 yards east of Charles Fort; it was started after the outbreak of the War of the Spanish Succession. By 1713 it consisted of a hexagon of massive walls enclosing an area of about an acre and a half of land, and could hold 300 men. Cooped up in a magazine without food or water, they could never have held out for long.

Although there was constant threat of attack on Barbados by the Spaniards and the French, it took events in England for fortification to be taken seriously. The English Civil War ended, King Charles I was executed, and England became a Commonwealth under Oliver Cromwell. Here in Barbados disagreements between Royalists and Parliamentarians increased. The Royalists faction gained the upper hand and exiled the Roundhead supporters of Parliament. Needless to say, Cromwell took military action to bring Barbados back into the Commonwealth.

Former Artillery Barracks and Band Block Garrison

In 1650, Lord Willoughby, the new Proprietor and Governor of Barbados, could see that Commonwealth forces would not tolerate the Royalist support on the island, and immediately strengthened the defences and trained and equipped the militia, which had been formed ten years previously. Every able-bodied free man was expected to serve and this included free coloureds but excluded slaves and indentured whites.

Property was a prerequisite for officers, the more property the higher the military rank. These officers had great social cachet, the planters and merchants always addressing each other by their military rank. When the defence of Barbados was put to the test during Sir George Ayescue's blockade and the invasion at Speightstown, Lord Willoughby was faced with the desertion of some of his prized militia troops and the day was won for Cromwell's Commonwealth.

In 1805 Barbados was once again threatened by French naval forces. However, a British fleet under Admiral Nelson, and his subsequent victory at Trafalgar in October that year, lifted the threat of invasion. The governor, Lord Seaforth, asked the British government to improve the long-term security of the island, and additional barracks for housing 800 more troops were constructed in three brick barracks east of the Savannah. They were completed by 1808.

The Stone Barracks at the Garrison circa 1913

At the end of the eighteenth century, which included the French Revolution in 1789 and the war with Revolutionary France, the Caribbean was the centre of operations and Barbados was at the centre of it all, providing the base for attacks on islands held by the enemy. All the troops in Barbados were ready for such expeditions or reserved as reinforcements for the defence of other British colonies, if threatened. In spite of all this, the Garrison failed to provide adequate housing for the officers and men. They were often under canvas in the Brittons Hill and Dayrells Road areas; sometimes reports had it that they were as far away as Oistins and Speightstown. A private in the Royal Scots Fusiliers reported that he had been sent to a mountainous area called Scotland.

Something had to be done, and the renewed outbreak of war with France in 1803 led to the expansion of the Barbados Garrison as headquarters for Britain's land forces in the Windward and Leeward Islands. Soon, 48 acres of land was purchased, extending into Lower Dayrells Road, taking in the land where the three brick barracks were later built. At the same time eight acres to the east of the Garrison was to be the site of a new General Hospital, started in 1803 and finished in 1806. During this time of expansion the Ordnance Hospital, ancillary buildings and two houses for medical staff were acquired. Gun Hill in St George and Moncrieffe in St Philip were used by the army as a refuge when epidemics of yellow fever raged at the Garrison.

THE DRILL HALL AND PART OF THE PARADE GROUND CIRCA 1915

In 1780, the decision was made to make a permanent British garrison in Barbados. There were ambitious plans to build a keep around it, making a fortified citadel. France and the newly independent United States of America declared war on Britain in June 1778. That same day, King Louis XVI dispatched orders directing the governor-general of Martinique to attack and take Britain's possessions in the West Indies. In spite of this new situation, the defences of Barbados did not change much.

Soon after the instructions from France arrived in Martinique, French forces invaded and captured Dominica; this was followed the next year by the taking of St Vincent and Grenada. After this it was clear that the French intended to capture Barbados next, and the British government sent regular troops here under Major General Sir John Vaughan, with Admiral Sir George Rodney in command of the naval forces in the West Indies.

The Barbados government was not even granted the courtesy of being told of these decisions. The first thing they knew was when General Vaughan arrived with the 89th Regiment and the whole party had to be billeted and fed as best as could be managed. No sooner had they settled in than the island was devastated by the 1780 hurricane. Not fazed by any of this, the troops continued to arrive on the island in large numbers.

By 1783, the American War of Independence had ended and the French threat seemed to have gone away, but there had to be some protection for the islands recently returned to Britain by the Treaty of Versailles, namely St Kitts, Nevis, Montserrat, Grenada, the Grenadines, St Vincent and Dominica.

THE MAIN GUARD, THE GARRISON CIRCA 1913

This picture shows the Main Guard, or central focus of the Garrison. Built in 1804 with its distinctive cupola tower, it bears the arms of King William IV, and a fine clock made by Dwerri and Carter in London. There is also a small guardhouse to the north of it. The Main Guard was used for, among other things, courts martial, with prisoners being kept in the guardhouse. Behind the Main Guard were the stables and the Quartermaster General's store houses. This later became the work shop of the Royal Engineers.

By the time the Garrison had been completed and at the height of its efficiency, in addition to the Main Guard and the Parade Ground, there were magazines, Officers' Quarters, Regimental Engineers' Quarters, Sergeants' Married Quarters and Married Non-commissioned Officers' Quarters. In fact, as many as 4,000 men and their dependants were quartered there. There was the Military Prison, the Military Chapel, the Ordnance Hospital and the Latrine and Ablutions Buildings (the privates were recommended to wash their feet twice a week!)

There were also stables, a Cook House, a Naval Magazine, Drill Hall, Signal Station, Rum Store, Military Cemetery, Dock Yard, Engineer's Pier and a tunnel leading from the Parade Ground up to St Ann's Fort. Brick gateposts are all that remain to mark the old gates of the Garrison. They are to be seen on Bay Street, Hastings Road, Dayrells Road and Dalkeith Road.

Volunteers at the Garrison Savannah circa 1872

The wars with France ended in 1815 and the function of the Garrison changed considerably. No longer the hub of offensive and defensive action, it still continued to be the headquarters of the Windward and Leeward Islands Command. The strength of the Garrison fell from approximately 2,700 troops in 1815 to fewer than 1,500 by 1854. From 1858 it consisted of one regiment, supplemented by a detachment of a West India regiment, and the function of various buildings started to change.

Now internal security became a problem. A slave insurrection in St Philip was put down in two days with the help of a British regiment. The white population wanted precautions to be taken against anything similar happening again, so the chain of signal stations manned by the Royal Artillery was established. The hurricane of 1831, which devastated the island, caused great damage to the Garrison and much effort was put into rebuilding it.

After emancipation in 1834 and the establishment of a police force, there was no need to have a militia and it disappeared by the 1860s. Some volunteer military organisations were formed in Barbados but only functioned from time to time. With the withdrawal of the British forces, the Barbados Volunteer Force came into being on 2nd July 1902. It performed its first ceremonial parade on the King's birthday in 1904. In 1907 some members of the force were sent to St Lucia as a result of disturbances there. During the First World War the Volunteer Force was mainly concerned with the defence of the island; however several members resigned to join various British regiments, where they served with great distinction.

A Day At The Races

Race day in Barbados eighty years ago and the Savannah is packed with spectators! Races were an eagerly anticipated event in an island starved of entertainment, and from early morning streams of people would assemble on the Savannah, walking in from outlying country districts. Men, women and children looked forward to the afternoon's entertainment. The races themselves caught everyone's attention, as is clearly shown in this photograph, but in between, people strolled about, patronizing the various nut sellers and other hucksters, or taking part in impromptu games of chance, or simply socializing.

Races in Barbados have a long history. Eighteenth century newspapers frequently advertise the holding of races on plantations. These were of course completely amateur events, but were taken quite seriously, with large bets being placed.

With the withdrawal of the British Garrison, the old parade ground or Savannah became available for organized racing, and the Barbados Turf Club was formed.

Saying Goodbye to the Last of the British Garrison from the Engineer's Pier, 13 November, 1905

The photographer captures the drama of an ending era. Centuries of warfare in the Caribbean between Britain and France, brought a strong military presence to Barbados, which became the southern headquarters of the British military in the Lesser Antilles. The Pax Victoriana and shifting British interests, coupled with the high cost of maintaining a garrison, caused the War Office in London to close their headquarters and withdraw their troops. This decision was met with local consternation because it meant economic loss for the island. Local elites also feared the loss of the British military presence which they perceived to be a stabilizing influence on the island.

Here the 4th battalion of the Worcestershire Regiment is embarking on the Troopship HMS Zaria which is accompanied by the warship HMS Diamond. The following year, the West Indian Regiment departed, leaving the island to fend for itself in defence matters.

A large crowd has assembled, women and men, to catch a glimpse of the departing troops. This is the age of the shared spectacle and oral culture. Radio and Television were unthought of dreams of the future. Stories of this day will reverberate in villages throughout Barbados, to be passed on to subsequent generations.

The Lock Hospital

In this picture a brave man stands outside the Lock Hospital to have his photograph taken. The Lock Hospital, or the Hospital for Contagious Diseases, came into being in 1866. Previously it had been a private residence, then a hotel. At that time, the British government passed an act "for the better prevention of Contagious Diseases at certain Naval and Military stations with the object of safeguarding members of the armed forces from venereal infection". The Secretary of State for the Colonies sent a copy to Barbados where there was a naval establishment and a large garrison, suggesting local modification.

The British government offered to contribute £2,500 towards building a hospital for the medical treatment of prostitutes, and to provide £625 p.a. towards the maintenance of 25 beds. In 1868 the Legislature passed the Contagious Diseases Act. The land was bought in Bay Street, and the hospital opened at a cost of £4,730, of which the Barbados government provided £2,230.

The Contagious Diseases Act required the registration, compulsory medical examination, and treatment if necessary of any woman reported as being a prostitute by a sergeant or corporal of the police force. The military and naval doctors treated the forces. At the time of opening, 449 women were registered; ten years later only 159. There had not been an improvement of moral or economic standards, but a lack of supervision; the total police staff engaged in this operation consisted of two policemen who also had other duties to perform.

After the repeal of the Act and the withdrawal of its grant, the hospital closed in 1887 and was allocated to the police, harbour police, and fire brigade. Unfortunately this late eighteenth century building was demolished in 1998.

THE HARBOUR POLICE PIER SHOWING BAY STREET IN THE BACKGROUND CIRCA 1900

This photograph attracts our interest for many reasons. It provides evidence of the cyclical nature of beaches in Barbados. One hundred years ago, the large and expansive Brown's Beach did not exist. In this photograph, the water laps the edge of properties fringing Carlisle Bay. Some of the buildings shown here have disappeared, such as the gasworks building with its large chimney. Others have survived and can be identified. One can see the Brick House and Marine Villa, the property now occupied by the Harbour Lights nightclub.

At the time this photograph was taken, the Esplanade had not yet been constructed. Another detail which deserves comment is the gas lamp placed at the end of the pier as gas lighting was still being used in Bridgetown. Remnants of this pier still survive. It was used by the Harbour Police which was started in 1867.

Bathing Pavilion and Engineers Pier circa 1900

After the withdrawal of the Royal Engineers at the turn of the century, the Engineers Pier was no longer required for their purposes. The Pier, along with 17 acres, was purchased by the Royal Mail Steam Packet Company, but it was left unused until 1910 when it was purchased from them by a group known as the Barbados Improvement Association, which intended it for the use of tourists, and it became known as the Bathing Pavilion.

The jetty remained much as the Engineers had left it, and the disused buildings became changing cubicles and a bar and restaurant. Very soon this was a popular meeting place for the middle-class white youths of Bridgetown. Given the social norms of the day, with its strict colour and class demarcations, blacks and poor whites were not welcome there.

THE AQUATIC CLUB CIRCA 1924

The popularity of the Bathing Pavilion led Mr Victor Parravicino and a group of friends, which included Mr Sam Manning, to acquire the site in 1924 and this became the Aquatic Club. It was entered off Bay Street and via the Cottage Gift Shop. The new owners added a two-storied building at the end of the jetty and painted the entire club in broad stripes of red and white. At the entrance was a ticket office where tickets could be purchased for the various facilities. There was a charge for the changing cubicles, and hire of bathing suits and towels (mostly required by visitors from the many ships at anchor in Carlisle Bay). There were hot dogs for sale, probably the first on the island. Upstairs was a cinema showing the latest films to reach the island. Benches were placed along the length of the jetty and this enabled onlookers (mostly girls) to watch the water polo or simply to see the action.

The new building at the end of the pier had various swings, ropes and slides that did much to enliven a sea bath and there was also a bar. Upstairs was an elegant dance floor, with a revolving mirrored dome suspended from the centre of the ceiling; this caught the light and scattered bright spangles over the dancers.

To the right of the Aquatic Club was the exclusive Royal Barbados Yacht Club. Most of its present members would not have been allowed to darken its doors at the time of this photograph. It operated a strict membership code, though not as strict as the more exclusive clubs of Pall Mall or St James in London. Membership at the Royal Barbados Yacht Club required an invitation to join, to be seconded, and then followed a five week period of free membership, for the members to decide if the candidate was suitable. Next at least fifty members of the club were required to vote; one negative vote needed six positive votes to over ride it. Failing this count the prospective member was considered "black balled". The ordinary citizens went to Browns Beach where they enjoyed themselves as much as any one else.

THE COTTAGE GIFT SHOP

The Cottage Gift Shop was situated on the right of the entrance to the Aquatic Club. It was run on the lines of the Women's Self Help, and in addition to beautifully hand-made and embroidered items of table linen and baby clothes, it sold old ornaments, toys and jewellery on commission.

THE CARNEGIE LIBRARY CIRCA 1911

A literary society was established in Barbados in 1777, and a Library Association in 1814. Both of these were private organisations and members paid to join.

In 1847 an Act was passed to establish a public library and a museum in Barbados. This was three years before a similar act was passed in Britain with regard to the library. The Literary Society and the Library Association donated their books, and the first public library was started in the house previously owned by William Codd in Coleridge Street. This house was known as the New Town Hall, but the library was small and run badly; by 1874 it was moved to the Public Buildings. The building of the new library, which is now also on Coleridge Street, was opened in 1904. It was paid for by the American philanthropist Mr Andrew Carnegie, on the understanding that it should always be a free library.

This library was and is a boon to the urban population of Barbados; an oasis of peace and quiet for the poorer classes of both races, for whom small accommodation and large families made study at home a near impossibility. Its facilities have always been grasped by a large number of intellectual and ambitious black people.

THE GENERAL HOSPITAL CIRCA 1911

The land for the General Hospital for the relief of the sick poor was purchased in 1839 and the hospital was established by private subscription in 1840.

It was an institution of which Barbadians could be justly proud. Liberally endowed by the Legislature, all goods imported by the directors, or purchased in bond for the hospital, were exempt from the payment of duties.

The hospital had three resident surgeons, these being Mr G.M. Manning M.D., C.M., Mr T.L.E.Clarke M.D., C.M. and Mr A.G. Bancroft M.D., C.M. The visiting surgeons were Mr F.G.W. Deane F.R.C.S., Mr E.H. Bannister M.B., C.M., and Mr R.M. Johnson L.R.C.S. The visiting physician was Dr W.B. Grannum L.R.C.S., and the ophthalmic surgeon the Hon. J.R. Phillips M.B., C.M. The head nurse was Miss A. Veecock, the chaplain the Rev. A.B. Williams, and the secretary was J.G.C. Ward. His Excellency the Governor was the president, the Bishop the deputy chairman and several distinguished members of the Legislative Council sat on the General Hospital Board. Life directors were Mr E.T. Racker and Mr J. Baeza.

THE CENTRAL ALMSHOUSE, ST MICHAEL, CIRCA 1913

This is a picture of the up-to-date institution that provided for the destitute poor of that parish. Each parish of the island had an almshouse for its "paupers", paid for by local taxes collected and administered by the vestry or parish council.

At this time there was also an excellent "lunatic asylum" at Black Rock, which had its own model farm, providing employment for its inmates. The asylum was built by the then Superintendent of Public Works, Mr Brady, from his own plans.

In St Michael there was also an extensive Lazaretto, built to house leprosy patients. This was also planned and built by another Superintendent of Public Works Mr Bowen.

THE TOWN HALL CIRCA 1911

The Public Magazine, which stored ammunition for the defence of the island and had been built in 1683, was demolished in 1728 to make room for a simple building to accommodate the Legislature, the Law Courts and the common gaol. Magazine Lane in lower Bridgetown helps us to position the spot.

The building cost the government £6,000. It was finished in 1730, but it took a further five years for the Provost Marshal to gain permission to transfer convicts to the cells. The Town Hall Gaol was sometimes used as a detention centre for prisoners-of-war. During the war with France, a number of French military prisoners were confined there from 1747 to 1748, and during the War of American Independence, 1776–1783, a large number of American, French, and Spanish prisoners were held there as well.

When William Codd's house was bought in 1837 as the "New Town Hall", the old Town Hall was simply called the Common Jail. In 1958 it became the Law Courts, and is still utilised for this purpose today.

Glendairy Prison circa 1911

The governor Sir W.M.C. Colebrooke laid the corner stone of Glendairy Prison on 2nd March 1853. By 1876 there was a decided improvement for prisoners in Barbados; the governor, Sir John Pope-Hennessy, put an end to the use of the underground cells of the Town Hall Gaol. These cells were used at that time for the incarceration of debtors.

The prison was divided into male and female sections. There were 275 cells for the male prisoners, and 128 cells for the females. The daily average number of prisoners during 1911 was 121 males and 82 females. There was only one death (from pneumonia).

The prison had a bakery, which baked bread for all the prisoners and also for the inmates of the lunatic and leper asylums.

At the time of this photograph the governor of the prison had the unfortunate name of Mr J.M. Lash. The chaplain was the Rev. H.A. Ansell, the surgeon E.H. Bannister M.B.C., and the visiting justices were J.G. Knight (barrister-at-law) and W.W. Gowdey.

Bush Hill House

This was the plantation house of Cogan's plantation owned by William Cogan, a merchant, and shown on maps as Cogans as early as 1722. Captain Richard Crofton, who was both Commander of St James Fort and a medical practitioner, married Cogan's daughter and owned it by 1746. Soon after his ownership, it was used as an approved house for 95 French prisoners. It was also used as a magazine for storing ammunition.

In 1751, it was rented by George Washington at the age of 19, on his only visit outside the United States. Barbados already had a good reputation as a healthy place for the winter, and was suitable for Washington's older brother Lawrence, who was suffering from tuberculosis. They stayed nearly seven weeks, during which time they were warmly received and entertained by their wealthy relatives on the island, as documented in George's diary. George Washington caught small pox here, which made him immune to the disease when it ravaged his revolutionary army during the American War of Independence. The outcome of the war might have been quite different had Washington not been immune.

In 1789 it was bought with 16 acres, together with an old windmill for pumping water, and a bathhouse, by the British Ordnance Department for the development of the Garrison, and became the quarters of the Commanding Officer of the Garrison.

There are plans by the Barbados National Trust to restore this building in conjunction with the Government of Barbados, both as a tourist attraction and a historical and genealogical interpretive site, explaining the many links between Barbados and the United States of America.

HOLBORN HOUSE CIRCA 1920

This was unquestionably one of the oldest houses on the island. Peter Campbell, in *Some Early Barbadian History,* notes that it must have been built in the 1640s and, by 1663, the then governor, Lord Willoughby, recommended that the House of Assembly use the property for the official residence of the governor. After the purchase of Pilgrim in 1692 as the governor's seat, Holborn reverted to private ownership, and survived three centuries with their dangers and natural disasters. It was last occupied by Mr Carlton Hill, a Bridgetown merchant and his family.

The front of this beautiful old house was shaded by an ancient evergreen tree. The flower garden was in the English style with numerous rose bushes and much sweet alicia and tuberoses.

To the east of the house was a well-tended tennis court. Behind the house were the stables and feed rooms, a coach house, laundry, servants' rooms, and wood store. Two arched verandas ran along the sides of the house; across the front was a terrace enclosed by low railings. A large arched door led to a wide hall which was laid with squares of dark grey and white marble. On the right hand wall was a sculpted marble plaque depicting Lyme Regis; this now hangs in the Barbados Museum. A large airy room led off the hall to the right; this was the main drawing room. On the other side of the hall on the left was a somewhat smaller sitting room or study. Behind the large drawing room was an enormous dining room and correspondingly on the other side of the hall was a smaller dining room or breakfast room. The stairwell was behind the breakfast room and the kitchen and other domestic offices led off from around the stairwell. Upstairs were five fine bedrooms.

With the construction of the Deep Water Harbour, which started in 1958, the house and land were acquired by an oil company and, sadly, this fine seventeenth-century structure in excellent condition was demolished to make way for oil storage tanks.

GOVERNMENT HOUSE CIRCA 1911

During the reign of Queen Anne, the mansion known as "Pilgrim" on the northern outskirts of Bridgetown, was made a residence for the officer administering the government. Prior to 1703 there were several early governor's houses in the seventeenth century: Doncaster House in Bay Street, and finally the house of the famous Colonel Walrond at Holborn in Fontabelle, but in 1698 Governor Grey refused to stay there as it was too low-lying.

Great Pilgrim House was a Quaker property; it was in a convenient position and leased for £120 per annum. Immediately it was lavishly stocked with several gross of bottled ale, Rhenish wine, and hogsheads of claret, for the arrival of Governor Granville.

The property was purchased by the government in 1736 for £1,350. It was extended and improved by Sir Thomas Robinson with such enthusiasm that he failed to obtain parliamentary approval and had to pay for the Robinson porch himself. More rebuilding work took place in 1755, and today it is much as it was then.

Both great hurricanes in 1780 and 1831 removed the roof. It was constantly being damaged and repaired and in 1836 to 1843, Hastings House next to the Marine Hotel was rented for the governor's use while repairs were made. The front of the house is the best of Barbadian Georgian architecture. It is large and grand, and the curved east wing may have inspired the facades of Bay Mansion, Villa Nova, and Farley Hill. Government House has welcomed many distinguished visitors both royal and political.

The gardens were large and beautiful, but both house and garden were treated as the home of the governor and his family. It was used for official entertaining, but at no time was it opened to the public prior to Independence in 1966.

A Wedding at Government House circa 1900

A large number of guests are assembled in this cleverly posed photograph of a wedding at Government House. The wedding party is posed on the steps of the billiard room located in the grounds of the Governor's residence. The Governor at the time this photograph was taken was Governor Probyn. To the right of the picture there is evidence of part of a marquee, no doubt for part of the reception. The costumes worn indicate that this is a turn of the century photograph. We can be sure that the invited guests represent the crème de la crème of Barbadian white society of the time. It was unusual for weddings to be held at Government House and this certainly indicates close ties between the Governor and the wedding party.

The bridegroom has been identified as the Danish Consul Mr Waldemar Hanschell, his bride is Miss Amy Manning. The Governor is seen in the background wearing his plumed helmet.

A Tram at Hastings Rocks

Although the trams were usually referred to as horse-drawn trams, the animals in this picture are clearly mules.

As early as 1851 the governor had submitted to the House of Assembly a scheme to establish tramways throughout the island. A committee of the House reported against the scheme on the grounds that it would cost £4,000 to £5,000 per mile.

In spite of this, the Barbados Tramway Company was started in March 1884. The tram travelled on rails and could not turn around, so the mules were simply hitched to the opposite end of the carriage for the return journey.

There were five tram routes, the fare being one penny per mile. The five routes comprised the Hastings, Fontabelle, Eaglehall, Roebuck and Constitution sections.

By the 31st July 1925, the trams were unable to compete with the motor buses and ceased to operate.

THE STANDARD ICE HOUSE HOTEL CIRCA 1911

The Standard Ice House stood at the corner of McGregor and Broad Streets. It was owned by an American, Mr D.P. Cotton, who was the first person to introduce a regular supply of ice and iced luxuries to Barbados from the United States of America in 1848.

The Ice House catered to the local and visiting middle class. The accommodation and food were excellent value.

Here is an interesting account of the Ice House by an American visitor in 1887: "...we reached an upper chamber, high and lighted by wide windows – all opened to admit the balmy trade wind – and had taken seats in a hall set about with easy chairs, where the clinking of glasses fell pleasantly upon the ear amid the sound of popping corks, the gurgling and fizzing of flagons; where there was a grateful, appetising odour of cooking. How I made merry with my friends... I found the Barbadians graduates in the science of hospitality, masters of the art of entertaining."

The Fresh Water Club

The Fresh Water Club was near to Black Rock, a lovely crescent of turquoise sea with fresh water springs bubbling up through the sand. It was a medium-priced hotel, well known for its dances, which took place in the airy ballroom, complete with a glittering rotating central globe hung from the ceiling, similar to the one at the Aquatic Club. Later it became known as the Paradise Beach Club.

The St Lawrence Hotel circa 1911

Mr J.C. Mahon was the proprietor at the time of this photograph of the St Lawrence Hotel, which was one of the two hotels on the St Lawrence Beach; the other one was known as the Bath Hotel. The modest St Lawrence Hotel was just to the east of the Anglican church named for the Saint. It was in a charming location and considered to have great advantages for those in poor health and in need of a seaside change.

The hotel was built on rocks and the bathing and accommodation were considered to be very fine. It was within five minutes' walk of the tram stop.

THE SEA VIEW HOTEL CIRCA 1911

The house known as Sheriff's House is of eighteenth-century brick, and as early as 1816 it is shown in a water colour of the Garrison. It first became a hotel in 1884 and, although it changed management many times, it was owned by the Gale family between 1889 and 1970.

This hotel was one of the most frequented on the island. Its popularity was due to its convenient and delightful situation, within easy reach of Bridgetown and the Hastings Rocks; there was excellent sea-bathing a short distance from the premises. The establishment was comfortable, the service competent and the cuisine first-class. At the time of this picture, Mrs I. Seon was the proprietress. During the occupation of the Garrison by British forces, a wooden building stood opposite it, where amateur dramatics were performed.

THE MARINE HOTEL CIRCA 1911

For 75 years, this hotel was reputed to be one of the finest health resorts in the tropics. Situated in Hastings village, about two miles from the Landing Place in Bridgetown, it had a tram-car connection two minutes from the hotel. The building was of limestone, and 360 feet long, with walls 30 inches thick and two large wings which contained 200 airy suites, with splendid views of the sea. The sea-bathing was considered suitable for the most delicate invalid; there were also private fresh water baths, both plunge and shower, within the hotel. Close by there was a stable connected to the hotel, where horses were available for riding, and carriages for hire at a moderate cost.

The Marine Hotel was the former Pomeroy Fine Hotel, named after its extrovert American owner, Mr Pomeroy. He played a major part in making Barbados known as a tourist and health resort. Its ornate cast-iron balconies, wide-sweeping verandas and huge ballroom were famous. The structure was said to have cost £15,000, a very large sum at that time.

Mr Pomeroy was a huge practical joker; when new visitors expressed surprise at the sophistication of the island, he obliged them by dressing some of his staff as "savages" and on another occasion as ghosts so that his guests could chance upon them while picnicking. Unfortunately, this beautiful hotel was demolished in 1996 to make way for a new hotel training school known as the "Pommarine".

The Crane Hotel circa 1920

The Crane Hotel opened in July, 1886. It was built on a cliff with sweeping views of the Atlantic, in what had been a small port before 1770. A small inlet through the reef, known as the Cobblers Rocks, led to the little port which had a crane for unloading goods; this gave the Crane its name.

Previously, it had been a large private residence called Marine Villa, believed to have been built in the late-eighteenth century. It was used throughout the nineteenth century as a bay house. The Crane, like Bathsheba, had a great reputation as a healthy seaside resort. In 1886 it was bought by Mr Donald Simpson and Co., enlarged and converted into a hotel. This was well timed as the new railway had opened in 1883 and made it accessible to holiday makers, both local and from abroad.

In 1911 Mr G.E. Carter was the manager, and the following is an advertisement of the time: "The Crane Hotel is a Seaside Resort for families, invalids and pleasure seekers. The fresh and invigorating air of the Atlantic restores health without the aid of Medicine. The bedrooms are all fitted with English Hair Beds and spring mattresses. The rooms are large and exceedingly cool. For a room and first class cuisine, terms are eight to ten shillings per day, long stay twelve dollars per week; special terms for families."

THE ATLANTIS HOTEL CIRCA 1911

The modest Atlantis Hotel at Tent Bay, Bathsheba, was one of the first hotels on the east coast, made possible by the new railway line. It was started by Miss Emmeline McConney and guests from Bridgetown could alight from the train just below its veranda. In the days of sail, watching the fishing boats return to Tent Bay was a superb sight together with the coming and going of the train and the long walks in the fresh air.

Miss McConney was an excellent proprietress, studiously considering the needs, comfort and cuisine of her guests.

THE BEACHMOUNT HOTEL CIRCA 1911

The Beachmount Hotel was originally the rectory for St Aidan's Church. St Aidan's collapsed into the sea during the construction of the railway line and had to be rebuilt. Beachmount liked to sell itself as a "home away from home". The meticulous Miss Emmeline McConney moved here with all the knowledge and experience of her guests at the Atlantis.

In the 1920s the hotel was owned by Mr Percy Roach, a Roebuck Street provision merchant. The top floor of the hotel was leased to a wealthy Quaker lady, a Miss Holt of the Lamport and Holt Steamship Company. This lady lived a quiet life, having her meals sent up on a tray; she often requested specific piano pieces to be played by Mr Roach's niece. This good lady taught a Sunday school near Horse Hill, and was reputed to have been jilted as a young woman. She is buried in the small cemetery near Joe's River, and the children she taught are now old men and women.

Good food, the relaxed atmosphere, sea bathing from High Rock and long walks made for happy holidays. Beachmount was a popular honeymoon hotel. A Mr Holder, in white mess jacket and gloves was the butler, and Mr Mayers the barman. In later years, Mr Mayers moved on from Bathsheba to become the barman at the Savannah Club in Port-of-Spain, Trinidad.

Chalky Mount

Chalky Mount in St Andrew rises from the beach to a height of 571 feet, with a distinctive and interesting geological formation. In this picture the old bay house known as "Benab" is in the foreground. Not shown is another bay house called "The Ark" which is made of Guiana green heart wood, which seems to become harder with age. Interestingly, the word "Benab" is an Guianese word for an Amerindian house built on stilts.

The potteries are situated to the back and on top of Chalky Mount. At the time of this picture, the potters would have charged a few cents for their pots, which ranged from plant pots to various jugs and bowls. The most distinctive was the monkey jar, used for keeping drinking water cool. Water would seep through the porous pottery and the constant evaporation would keep the contents cool. The monkey jar undoubtedly came from West Africa, where similar jars are still in use.

At the turn of the century, Mr Devonish was the master potter of the area; he lived at the foot of Chalky Mount in those days, but his descendants now live on top of Chalky Mount, enjoying some of the most superb views on the island.

The Potteries

In this photograph, a potter removes a pot from an underground kiln. In the background is part of Chalky Mount Village. Today, such primitive kilns are not used. A potting industry has existed on the island since the seventeenth century.

The clay was dug out of Chalky Mount manually. It was soaked in water for two days, during which time it absorbed the correct quantity of water; this is the part of the technique that required long experience. The potter then used his feet to tread the clay to the right consistency. It was parcelled out into manageable lumps and covered with wet crocus bags.

The next step was a two-person operation. The potter's wheel was attached to a firm base by a small crank shaft; a stick was attached to this, and one person turned the wheel at a steady pace while the other threw the clay on the wheel and turned the pot. When this was completed, the wet pot was removed from the wheel by a length of string. The correct temperature in the kiln could only be gauged by long experience. This heat had to be maintained for 15 minutes, then the kiln was allowed to cool slowly overnight to prevent the pottery from cracking.

Stacking Clay Pots

A lady receives some pots from an underground kiln, which have been handed to her by the man who is standing in the entrance to the kiln. In the foreground are monkey jars, flower pots, pots with pinched edges, small bowls used for food preparation, and tall Conaree jars which are still used for Pepperpot and were also used for the salting and storing of fresh meat when animals were butchered.

These clay pots would have cooled down in the kiln overnight; as they were being stacked, they would be checked for cracks and imperfections and those that were rejected would be broken on the spot.

Pottery on the Careenage

Here a lady looks at the pottery for sale on the Careenage. She is beautifully dressed in Edwardian clothes, and a straw boater. Her small waist was almost certainly achieved by wearing a corset; these were worn, in spite of the heat, by women who could afford them. She carries her neatly wrapped purchases by a string.

This large selection of pottery would have arrived in Bridgetown, packed in boxes and trays of dry sour grass. Before there was a train from Belleplaine, it would have had to make the journey to Bridgetown on people's heads and by mule cart.

THE BARBADOS MUTUAL LIFE ASSURANCE BUILDING CIRCA 1911

This ornate late-Victorian building was built between 1894 and 1895. It faces east towards Beckwith Place, and was designed by the English firm of architects, Messrs. Cossin and Peacock, and was constructed by Mr C.J. Greenidge, who had previously built the St Michael's Almshouse. The beautiful iron work on the building was imported from Birmingham, Leeds and Glasgow. This building is unquestionably one of the most striking buildings of Bridgetown.

The Interior of the City Pharmacy, Knight's Limited

In addition to its function as druggists and chemists, this well-established pharmacy sold many items – cosmetics, sea sponges, honey, home-made jam, and sweets. It also had an American style "Soda Fountain", where ice creams and ice-cream sodas could be bought.

Cave Shepherd Wholesale Provision Store circa 1906

Up to 1907, Mr P.G. Cave and Mr J.P. Shepherd with a third partner ran this provision business in Palmetto Street. Next door to this building was their bonded warehouse. Messrs Cave and Shepherd gained their business experience in the provision trade. From quite an early age, they worked as salesmen, handling numerous Canadian and American products, mainly flour, meal, oats, corn, hay, rice, peas, beef and pork, on a large scale. Supplying cattle feed to planters was a prominent feature of their business; their Canadian oats were well known as "Planters A1".

Their aptitude for business, understanding of accounts, and the fact that they were both well known and liked in the community won the confidence of their employers and they ultimately became managing directors of the firm W.L. Johnson and Co. Ltd. In 1906, when they decided to start trading under their own names, they were well equipped to do so. Seeing the opening for a quality store in Broad Street, after much deliberation, they started to search for suitable premises.

CAVE SHEPHERD AND COMPANY, "THE IDEAL STORE", BROAD STREET, CIRCA 1911

A small book of 1911 describes "The Ideal Store" as follows:

> *"The front of the store has fine large and elaborately decorated glass cases, so skilfully decorated is each case, that it could be described - to use a figure of speech - as a poem. To walk through "The Ideal Store" is comparable to making a tour of some gorgeous glade, richly dowered by nature in a lavish mood."*

Needless to say, Cave Shepherd and Company had published this book, and it certainly shows that their advertising ideas were also excellent!

Once the decision had been made to open the store, a Mr Waite was employed as their buyer. A building in Broad Street was purchased from the defunct firm Ramsay, Elder & Co. and soon extensive structural and modernisation work was in hand. At this point Mr Waite sailed for Europe on his first buying trip. There he immediately used his 30 years of marketing experience in Barbados; his critical choice was excellent in buying good quality at reasonable prices. As his terms of purchase were always on a cash basis, Mr Waite was able to stock up with some marvellous bargains. During his many buying trips, he made lasting and valuable connections with reliable suppliers in London, Manchester, Bedfordshire, Nottingham, Paris, Hamburg, and New York. From the day it opened, the store was a success.

THE BONNET ROOM, "THE IDEAL STORE", CIRCA 1911

The Bonnet Room was considered to be a microcosm of the milliner's art – collected by Mr Waite with great taste. Hats and bonnets could be purchased trimmed or untrimmed; of the trimmed ones, no two were ever alike. Artificial flowers, feathers, veils, and other ornaments for hats were also available.

The many departments in this store included a Gents Furnishing Department, selling an assortment of woollens, tweeds and flannels, and offering an excellent bespoke tailoring service. Other departments were Cotton Drapery, Ladies Dress Goods, Boots and Shoes, Haberdashery, Sewing Machines, a Ready-Made Clothing section, Hosiery, Underwear, and a Corset Department which stocked 19 brands of corsets which promised to "impart grace and symmetry, even to the abnormal figure, all shaped on nature's perfect lines".

THE FANCY GOODS DEPARTMENT, "THE IDEAL STORE", CIRCA 1911

In this picture the sales ladies are ready to serve the customers. Notice the small cash boy in front of the counter. These boys from very poor homes joined the stores at the age of eight or nine years old; in an urban society it was one of the ways their parent (usually a widow) could feed them. Their function was to take the bill and cash to the cashiers and return with the receipt and change. This department sold decorated combs, hair and hat pins, handbags, pocket handkerchiefs made of lawn, Irish linen or soothing silk. There were high-quality gloves in kid, suede, lisle, washing castor, and cotton. In addition there were parasols, umbrellas and sunshades.

For lady customers only, the store provided a lavatory and luncheon room on the second floor. Here, after the bustle below, ladies from the rural districts could wait before going to the railway station; also those awaiting a tram car or private carriage were invited to avail themselves of this boudoir.

THE COUNTING HOUSE, "THE IDEAL STORE", CIRCA 1911

This is a picture of the counting house which was on the first floor of "The Ideal Store". In this picture, facing each other across a desk, are two of the partners Mr R.G. Cave, facing the camera, and Mr C.S. Waite facing him. The third partner, Mr J.P. Shepherd, was at the time enjoying a short and well-earned holiday in Canada. One of the lady clerks behind the rails is busy typing while another is on the telephone. Two of the gentlemen clerks are busy over their ledgers, while the third may well have been asked by the photographer to face the camera.

The sound business done here allowed the clear principle of profit-sharing with the customers. The company at this time employed approximately 50 members of staff. It was their written policy that their staff should be courteous and accommodating to all classes of their clientele, and to take pains to satisfy both the working classes as well as those in high positions in society.

Among the many urgent demands of his business, Mr Cave found the time to be a member of the St Michael's Vestry, a director of the Barbados Mutual Life Assurance Society and he was also a member of the Council of the Barbados Chamber of Commerce.

The Colonnade circa 1911

Mr David Da Costa bought out his partners at Barrow and Dummett in 1868. He started his own business which was known as Da Costa and Co. Universal Suppliers, and the fine two-storied building in Broad Street became known as the Colonnade.

Mr Da Costa of Sephardic Jewish origin, was a man of high principles. He had considerable political influence as well. He was one of the esteemed band of "Defenders of the Constitution" in 1876-1877 when the governor, Sir John Pope Hennessy, was trying to promote Confederation of the West Indies. By this, the Leeward and the Windward Islands would have federated and Barbados would have have had to give up her ancient rights and become a Crown Colony, like some of the other British Colonies. It is on record that the governor offered Mr Da Costa a knighthood if he would back Confederation, but Mr Da Costa indignantly refused the offer.

He finally retired in 1877 to London, where his house became the Mecca for Barbadians in London.

The Linen and Cotton Goods Department, Colonnade, circa 1911

This department was on the ground floor of the building. It stocked the finest quality linens, calicoes, sheeting, and prints imported from Great Britain and Ireland.

This department also sold honeycomb towels and bath sheets, choice bedspreads, damask napkins, tray and sideboard cloths, tablecloths in every size and shape, cushion cases and curtains.

Where the linen department ended, woollens, tweeds, and serges began. It is difficult to understand why there would have been a demand for these fabrics in Barbados, but it has to be remembered that men thought nothing of ordering a bespoke tweed suit, girl's school uniforms were usually made of serge, and seamstresses ran up daring bathing suits made from alpaca wool; that wool did not cling or reveal when it was wet. When trimmed with white braid, it turned into quite a fetching little number.

THE REFRESHMENT ROOM, DA COSTA'S, CIRCA 1911

The Refreshment Room at the Colonnade was run in conjunction with the grocery, and the grocery department was huge. In 1911 the population of Barbados was 200,000, dependent to a large extent on imported foodstuff, and all the ships in port had to be supplied. Half the amount of salt fish alone imported on the island was brought in by Da Costa's. The Refreshment Room was comfortable, well-ventilated and lighted, and made all customers welcome with polite service.

In addition to this, by 1911, electric ceiling-fans had been installed. In these comfortable surroundings the customers could order tea or coffee, cakes, ice cream, chocolate creams, lemonade, sweets, aerated drinks and choice liquors. Needless to say, it was a very popular venue in Bridgetown. The bakers, pastry cooks, and confectioners had access to the best-quality ingredients, and also had first-class reputations. The most expensive baking ovens in the West Indies were at the Colonnade.

With their reasonable prices and scrupulous attention to cleanliness, their products were much sought after and the output of the bakery was immense.

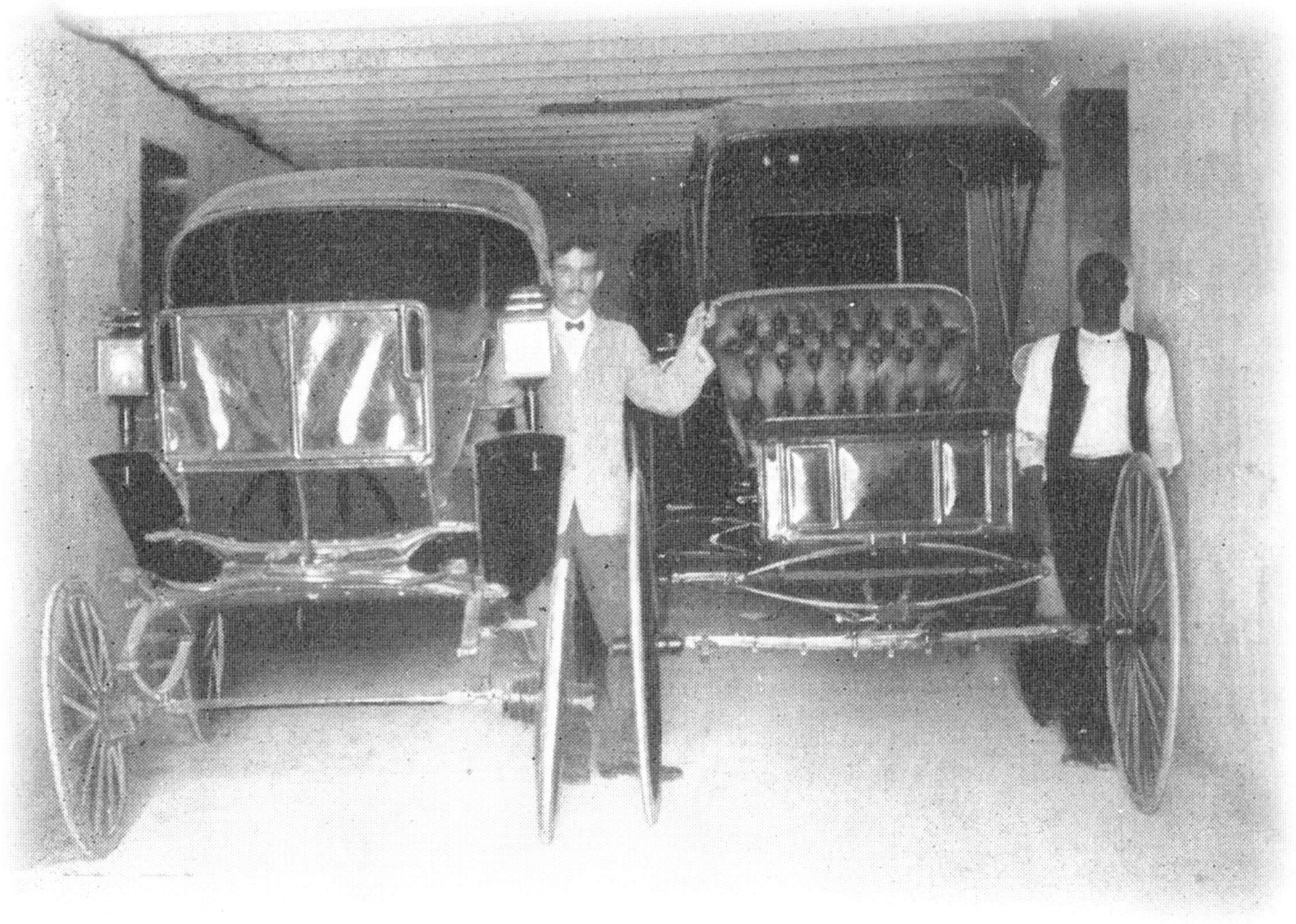

The Carriage Warehouse circa 1911

By 1911 Barbados probably had more vehicular traffic per capita than anywhere else in the West Indies. Vehicles suitable for horses, mules or donkeys had to be found, and Da Costa's could supply everything from a baby's pram to the brougham carriage, single and double buggies, gigs, wagons, dog carts, carriages of various designs and builds, including the much-favoured Victoria.

All these vehicles were paid for with spot cash from the finest builders in England, the United States, and Canada. They boasted the best-quality woodwork, springs and axles; there was also a choice of rubber or steel tyres. All had beautiful upholstery and trimmings. No other carriage warehouse on the island could compete with Da Costa's, and in addition to this the best leather was used for the manufacture of harness and saddles.

PORTION OF THE COMMISSION OFFICE, DA COSTA AND CO. CIRCA 1911

Before his retirement, Mr Da Costa had engaged in inter-colonial trade, mostly with St Vincent, Saba and Grenada. Merchants in Antigua, St Kitts, St Martin, Guadeloupe and St Lucia ordered their stock from Da Costa's, and Surinam (a Dutch colony) also engaged in large business with his firm.

All this commerce was undertaken by a fleet of schooners, and the Liverpool Steamship Company, the Leyland Line, sent their great ships to the West Indies as a direct result of Mr Da Costa's encouragement and business. The agency was given to him, and remained with him for many years.

He also rendered an immense service to the sugar interests on the island, liberating the planters from the representatives of two American firms, Platt, Dwight and Co. and Trowbridge and Co.; he opened the sale of Barbadian sugar and molasses to the open New York market. This proved to be of vital importance to the planters; their first question on reaching Bridgetown on Fridays was "What is Da Costa and Co. doing?"

Owing to Mr Da Costa's brilliance as a businessman, the Company now embraced every branch of commercial enterprise. On his retirement, Mr W.P. Clarke, his son-in-law, who had joined the business in 1886, together with three of his sons Darnley, Dudley and Ernest, not only took over his work but his great interest in public affairs on the island.

Sugar Cane Fields, Scotland District

Three planters, James Holdip, William Hilliard and James Drax, made sugar a commercial enterprise in Barbados. Once they had discovered the secrets of the growth and the manufacture, sugar dominated life in Barbados for the next 300 years.

The history of sugar cane dates from antiquity. Many areas of the world claim to be its place of origin. India or China are recognised as the origin of its cultivation, but its botanical origin appears to be Papua, New Guinea.

Ancient literary references seem to support India's claim for its cultivation. The word sugar derives directly from the Sanskrit "sakara"; centuries later it appears as "sukkar" in Arabic, subsequently as "saccharum" in Medieval Latin, and finally as sugar in Middle English.

Its cultivation would appear to have spread from India to China; island travellers carried it further east to the Philippines, Java and even Hawaii. As early as 700 AD Nestorian monks in the Euphrates region (now Iraq) successfully produced white sugar through the purifying action of ashes. Arabs spread its cultivation through North Africa to Southern Europe. It was manufactured commercially in Egypt during the 9th century, but it was not until "the Age of Discovery" of the Americas that it became available in large quantities and ceased to be a scarce luxury dispensed by apothecaries.

Christopher Columbus is said to have introduced it to the New World from Madeira on his second voyage to the Americas.

JOES RIVER PLANTATION CIRCA 1898

This picture shows a typical plantation on the eastern side of the island. The plantation house is surrounded by fields of young canes and ground provisions. The mill and boiling house are to the right, and in the foreground are some stone huts, formerly used by slaves, and chattel houses, situated in what was known as a tenantry. Joes River House was demolished early this century.

For some years after settlement, the chief crops exported from Barbados were indigo dye, cotton, ginger and aloes (for making purges in Europe). Before the island was completely deforested, the settlers were also able to export several types of wood. By 1640 the cultivation of canes and the manufacture of sugar was established. From then on it dominated life on the island for the next three hundred years.

A sad tale exists of the early deaths of the owners of this plantation in the eighteenth century, leaving a small son and heir. His uncle moved into Joes River House as the boy's legal guardian and he was placed in the care of a nurse. Both boy and nurse disappeared and the factory workers reported hearing cries and screams at night. On the demolition of the house, the skeletons of a small child and an adult were found bricked into a thick wall.

Sugar Cane Cultivation at Oistins (Formerly Austins)

Thick-stemmed "noble canes" had been brought to the West Indies by the English and the French in the late-eighteenth century; Bourbon was the most commonly planted. By the late 1800s red rot disease was rampant, and different types of canes were being brought in to replace Bourbon. No one thought that canes could set seeds, because the Bourbon variety had become sterile.

In 1859 an overseer at Highlands Plantation, called Irenaeus Harper, noticed some grass-like seedlings and showed them to his employer, Mr J.W. Parris. Irenaeus Harper had been observant enought to notice that the edges of this "grass" were sharper than the other grasses and similar to sugar cane.

Mr Parris realised the potential of this discovery and reported it in the Liberal newsaper, but little notice was taken of it at the time. Mr Parris was so convinced of the importance of the find that he transplanted the seedlings until he had four-and-a-half acres of them.

In January 1888, J.B. Pilgrim, a worker on an experimental plot at Dodds Reformatory School, reported fine grasses of a completely different variety growing near the cane plot. This time J.B. Harrison, then professor of chemistry and agricultural science, and J.R. Bovell, the agricultural superintendent were called in. They identified the seedlings as cane and transplanted and identified their characteristics. They also collected seed from the arrows and started to grow them.

As so often happens in science, similar discoveries had been made about this time in Java, so Barbados shares the honours with Java as the first two countries to initiate a sugar-cane breeding programme.

Cane Being Harvested and Drawn by Bullock Cart circa 1910

In this picture a field of sugar cane is being harvested. The cane was chopped off at ground level by a billhook; the green leaves are struck from the top of the cane, and the hook at the top of the bill is used for running down the stalk of cane to clean it of dry trash. This is necessary as the fields are not burnt in Barbados prior to harvesting as they are in other parts of the world to get rid of the trash and vermin. There are no poisonous snakes on the island, the soil is so thin that the cane tops are necessary to make mulch for the young canes, and with such small acreage for the growing of canes, burning is also thought detrimental to the quantity and quality of sugar produced. In addition the small factories on the island were not capable of grinding large quantities of burnt canes quickly, and normally the cane cutters and the mills worked together in a set rhythm.

Canes to Mill in Mule Carts and Ox Carts

Prior to mechanised transportation, all the canes were taken to the factory by mule or oxen carts.

Livestock was considered a necessity on a plantation prior to the use of chemical fertilisers. Their manure was carefully spread on the fields and, together with grass and dry trash, this was a very necessary method of fertilisation and water conservation on the thin, dry soils of the island.

In addition to the mules and oxen, there were milch cows and horses, pigs and chickens all helping to fertilise the cane and gardens on the plantations.

LABOURERS HEADING CANE TO THE MILL

In this picture we see an example of the intensive work which was needed in the production of sugar on the island. These men took a small load of canes on their heads from the mill yard to feed the rollers of the mill. It was necessary to grind the canes as soon as possible after they were cut, or they lost much of their sugar content.

One unique and remarkable fact about the sugar industry in Barbados is that its factories remained one size for many years. At the start of the industry the factories were of the then normal size; Barbados maintained its production with no increase in the size of its factories or departure from its primitive agricultural methods for many years. The movement towards larger factories and the use of steam and vacuum boiling was not implemented by Barbados for a long time. It became a colony of self-contained properties, of individual proprietors, and still kept a substantial degree of prosperity.

As late as 1913 there were 255 sugar works on the island, 159 ground their canes by windmills, and only 97 used steam.

Labourers Feeding a Sugar Mill

These structures are an integral feature of the Barbadian landscape. The cane was brought to the mill yard, then dumped on the ground. Labourers fed small bundles of cane into the mill between the metal rollers which were driven by the wind in the sails of the mill. Usually, the cane was passed through the rollers twice to extract the juice which was then conveyed in open gutters to the boiling house.

The windmills were always well placed to catch a good breeze. The canvas "sails" were fixed to the arms during the crop season, but removed out of crop. Each mill had a "tail tree" which enabled two oxen or mules to turn the whole superstructure or "house" of the mill to face into the wind at all times.

Sometimes accidents happened in the mill and a hand or foot was caught between the metal rollers. The appalling necessity of having to keep a cane bill in the mill to sever the trapped limb as soon as possible saved some lives, as there was absolutely no mechanism to bring the mill to an immediate stop.

A Typical Plantation House St Thomas circa 1918

This picture shows the comfortable lifestyle some planters derived from sugar, with gracious houses in good positions to catch the winds. A house like this had 75 acres of cane.The points of the windmill can be seen stacked in the yard. Now half of this house has been demolished, the out-buildings derelect, and the cane fields run to grass.

In addition, the plantation house had a large cellar that was used as a hurricane shelter for all the plantation workers in times of peril. There was a flower garden to the front and side of the house. Behind the house were mature fruit trees, several types of mangoes, paw paws, guavas, cherries, sapodillas, sugar apples, star apples, golden apples and mammy apples. There was also a well-stocked kitchen garden.

At the time of this picture the term “Great House” was not in common use, but was used in the tenantries. The plantation houses were simply referred to as Bushy Park House, Warrens House etc. Tenantries were built by the ex-slaves after emancipation on marginally productive plantation land. These tenants did not own the land and had to pay a rent for the house plot, but plantation owners reserved the right to evict them at short notice. The chattel house was the tenants answer to this dilemma; it could be dismantled, moved and reassembled if the tenant was forced to move on. Undoubtedly the gap between these two lifestyles was the cause of much dissatisfaction.

A Representative Field Gang on a Plantation

This photograph is representative of the three sets or classes of labourers, usually called gangs, that worked on the plantations. The first gang consisted of the most healthy and robust men and women. Out of crop this gang had to clear the ground, dig cane holes, and plant the cane. In crop time, they had to cut canes with a cane bill, load carts, feed the mill, and attend to the boiling of the juice.

The second gang was made up of young boys and girls, older labourers, heavily pregnant women, and convalescents. This gang was mostly employed to weed between the canes and other work suitable to their age and condition.

The third gang consisted of young children attended by a careful old woman. They were mostly employed in picking green plants for sheep and pigs, weeding kitchen and flower gardens, or other light tasks "to preserve them from habits of idleness". In addition to these three gangs, plantations would have domestic servants, carpenters, coopers and masons.

As pointed out earlier, Amerindians and Europeans found it very difficult to perform this heavy labour in intense heat (the height of the cane blocks out the majority of the breeze). The Africans with their superior strength and stamina were able to do this work. People of other ethnic origins also did this manual work of sugar cultivation; for example Chinese, Malayan and East Indians, to name a few. In the Western Hemisphere, African slaves and indentured East Indians were mostly used. In 1817, Queensland, Australia, became the last of the great sugar-producing areas to establish the culture. It is the only area of the world where sugar production is carried out exclusively by white men, but in a temperate climate and with early mechanisation.

A Mill Gang

Most of the people in this photograph would have worked in the first gang. In the crop season they took their turn to work in the mill.

The production of sugar was very labour intensive and consequently a large labour force was recruited. Barbadian planters were traditional and conservative, but they also had practical reasons for this; as long as there was no alternative to cutting canes manually by wielding a cane bill, labourers had to be kept busy out of crop time as well. Indentured and slave labour was well suited for this as the labour force could not move on after the harvest.

Barbadian planters continued for a long time in wasteful labour practices to occupy their labourers out of crop season: the hoe and fork were always used instead of the plough; dung was carried in baskets instead of a cart; and the squaring of cane holes persisted in Barbados long after the practice had been abandoned elsewhere. After slavery ended in 1834, a variety of laws were passed designed to coerce labourers to remain on the plantations.

INSIDE A BOILING HOUSE

It is easy to imagine the heat and steam and smell of cane syrup in this confined space. An overseer in a felt hat sits at his desk with his ledgers; the owner or manager is well turned out in a three-piece suit and a bowler hat regardless of the heat. Two little boys have come into the boiling house, drawn there as little boys would be. The mill gang stops to look at the camera; the scene is frozen in time for us.

As early as 1638, Colonel Drax and a couple of his friends had brought a Dutch planter from Brazil to help them to overcome their production difficulties. They learned to plant their canes by laying them in shallow trenches instead of upright in holes. They discovered that canes took 16 months to ripen, and that there was a proper way of cutting them. They learned the secret of how to extract the maximum amount of juice by drawing the canes twice through rollers. At first the canes were crushed by vertical rollers powered by bullocks and oxen. The more efficient windmills, patterned after Dutch designs, stood on a high flat point on the plantation, better to catch the wind, and so that the juice could run down to the boiling house, usually in open gutters. The raw juice was tempered by ashes dampened with water and another pipe led it to the first of five coppers or tayches; this was later reduced to three. The boiling liquor passed through each of these coppers becoming ever more concentrated, undergoing skimming and then ladling from one tayche to another. Finally the liquid was run off from the final round copper and collected in a rectangular cistern, where it was allowed to cool for three days and two nights.

This process was energy efficient and a good example of the complete utilisation of raw materials. The squeezed cane stalks were used to fire the furnaces of the boiling house and the ashes were used as fertiliser for the cane fields.

Boiling the Cane Juice

The production of raw cane sugar by open kettle boiling methods changed little through the centuries. The invention of the vacuum pan by E.C. Howard in England about 1813 was an enormous step forward in processing a heat-sensitive material such as sugar. Vacuum boiling spread rapidly from English refineries to other branches of the industry. All modern sugar boiling takes place in vessels similar to the type that Howard introduced.

The use of granular bone char for the decolourisation of refinery liquors was another innovation of that period. As an outgrowth of Howard's patent, in 1845 Norbert Rillieux, a free man of colour in Louisiana, built the first multiple effect evaporator for concentrating cane juice, resulting in savings in fuel, labour and sugar and that revolutionised the raw sugar process. The plate and frame filter press were other developments of this general period. All these scientific and technical advances, which the sugar industry pioneered, were later adapted or modified for other unrelated industries.

Oscillating Sugar

Here a woman stands on a large bench to oscillate the sugar. She turns the spokes, to which were attached canvas paddles; the paddles were rotated slowly so that the crystals of sugar were constantly brought into contact with the massecuite (a mixture of molasses and sugar crystals). This had the added advantage of cooling the massecuite, thus enabling optimum sucrose to be absorbed by the sugar crystals.

Sugar refining began as a small unit operation, depending on several boilings for purification by re-crystallisation. In the seventeenth, eighteenth and nineteenth centuries, hundreds of refineries dotted the larger ports of Europe and Great Britain. The final product was moulded into a cone and hardened by baking. Barbados was prohibited by British law from refining sugar, because refined sugar was worth more and they wished to make a profit from it themselves. However, as this eighteenth century account shows, some refined or clayed sugar was produced: “They then have clay finely mixed in water to the consistence of a good Batter. This is poured over the top of the sugar and is called claying it. The water passing through the sugar carries with it the coarser, drossy part, greatly purifies it from its Brown colour and much whitens it.”

The Barbados Rum Refinery

Rum is a by-product of sugar and, like sugar, the concept of its manufacture was brought to Barbados from Brazil. Barbadian rum was described by the historian Ligon as "the strongest Spirit or Liquor that is potable". Everyone drank it, especially the planters; but those who could afford it also bought imported English spirits or French brandy.

At first, rum was made from the scum that rose when the cane juice was boiled; later when molasses was used there was a great improvement. A further improvement was the practice of ageing the rum in old whisky casks. In the eighteenth century, rum was beginning to be distilled from cane juice, rather than from molasses. Barbadian planters did well out of this boom; the good ones covered their routine plantation expenses from the sale of rum, so their sugar was clear profit.

Both pot-still and continuous-still rums were made, still rum being the lighter. All rum is colourless when first distilled. The dark rums are aged in oak barrels with a small addition of caramel. White rum is supposed to cause no hangover, but many prefer the flavour of aged coloured rum. The most important thing is that the best rum comes from Barbados and that is the unanimous opinion here!

The Final Product

This picture shows wet sugar being weighed in hogsheads prior to shipment to Europe. Wet sugar is a mixture of sugar and molasses. The heavy hogsheads were weighed on scales which consisted of two A frames connected by a bar. This bar supported the scale which was known as a steelyard.

The hogsheads had to be weighed because it was difficult to gauge the contents. There were men whose profession it was to gauge the quality and density of the syrup once it was in the casks (puncheons or barrels). These men had to be well trained and experienced before being gazetted. There were only three or four men gazetted on the island at any one time.

Leaving for Panama from the Pierhead

Thousands of Barbadians emigrated to work on the construction of the Panama Canal. Between 1904 and 1914, one-third of the Barbadian population, or approximately 60,000 people, were estimated to be working there. The Canal was constructed between 1880 and 1914 as a vital facility for increased international trade. The Canal saved ships from having to sail thousands of miles through treacherous seas around Cape Horn (the furthest point south on the South American continent).

The workers were employed by the United States-controlled *Isthmian Canal Commission* and theirs was a life of hard work, most of it done with a pick and shovel. The conditions were very poor, the workers suffered discrimination and a high death rate from accidents and disease, especially yellow fever. In spite of all this, they were able to earn higher wages than in Barbados, and some survived to return with money to buy houses, land and businesses. This enabled their families to be independent of the plantation system, but more importantly it allowed many to qualify for the right to vote. The franchise which allowed this was based on property ownership and income, among other things, and these newly qualified people would start to change Barbadian politics forever.

Two-thirds of these workers did not return to Barbados; many settled in Cuba, the United States and Canada; some stayed in Panama where they form a unique addition to that population. The real work on the Canal started during the presidency of Theodore Roosevelt, and on a visit to Barbados in 1913,he publicly thanked the Barbadians for their help in its construction, emphasising the service it would render to mankind in general.

Warrens House, St Michael

This is one of the known seventeenth-century plantation houses in Barbados. It has the date 1686 inscribed over a veranda. From approximately 1674 to the 1730s the plantation was owned by the Sutton family, who were Quakers.

Warrens House took its name from its next owner, Robert Warren, who lived there from 1735. George Washington was invited to dine here during his visit to Barbados in 1751. Other owners included an MP, Dr Samuel Hinds, and Mr George Hewitt, who was something of a political personality in St Thomas. He fathered a coloured son, James Hewitt, who was educated at Oxford and became MP for St Thomas.

For many years the plantation was owned by the Challenor family and the house became the home of the plantation manager, the factory manager living in a smaller house close to the sugar factory.

DRAX HALL, ST GEORGE

Drax Hall is the oldest of the three surviving Jacobean houses in the Western Hemisphere. Nicholas Abbey in St Peter, and Bacon's Castle in Virginia are the other two. A length of copper guttering dates the house at 1653. Jacobean is the period between the Tudor and Georgian styles of architecture, starting in the reign of King James I of England.

Drax Hall is a typical Jacobean house with steep gables, stone corner finials, a Jacobean staircase, and an arched hall of mastic wood.

There is some uncertainty as to whether the house was built by James Drax or his son Henry Drax. They were both enormously wealthy, but the father returned to England where he was knighted the year after the house was completed.

It was on this plantation that Colonel James Drax first tried to cultivate sugar cane commercially. The Draxes were famous for their grand lifestyle and extravagances, well recorded by both Ligon and Bridenbaugh.

Nicholas Abbey, St Peter

Nicholas Abbey is the second Jacobean house in Barbados. It is believed that it was built by one Benjamin Berringer some time between 1656 and 1661.

Berringer, a wealthy planter and land speculator, was joint owner of this plantation with a John Yeaman. There was great enmity between the two men over Berringer's wife, in the course of which Yeaman was supposed to have had Berringer poisoned. Letters from the then governor, Lord Willoughby, mention this fact, and Mr Yeaman did in fact marry Mrs Berringer. In spite of all this, the property was inherited by Mr Berringer's son, and then by his granddaughter, Susanna. She, in turn, married a Mr George Nicholas and, as the law stood at that time, the plantation automatically became her husband's, and so it took his name.

In 1746 Sir John Gay Alleyne, the eminent baronet, planter and legislator, went to live there. He too had acquired it through marriage; he died there in 1801. It is believed that Sir John planted the magnificent mahogany avenue leading from Nicholas to Cherry Tree Hill. His son, Sir Reynold Abel Alleyne, is reputed to have ridden a horse up the staircase for a bet. A young lady was involved somehow and was supposed to have caused this escapade.

By 1816 the plantation was in Chancery, where it was bought by two Cumberbatch brothers. It is still owned by a Cumberbatch descendant, Colonel Stephen Cave.

There is absolutely no religious reason why it should be called an abbey, which is probably a bit of additional Victoriana.

The house is most attractive, with Dutch gables and corner chimneys. The arched portico, the cedar panelling, and the Chinese Chippendale staircase were added later; however the chimneys, fireplaces and walled herb garden were probably carefully copied from the original plans brought out from England.

Sam Lord's Castle

Samuel Hall Lord (1778–1844) was a planter and something of a rogue. He built this Regency house with castellations, superb staircases, and double verandas on all four sides. Charles Rutter and his two Italian assistants, who had all worked on the ceilings of Windsor Castle, are responsible for the gorgeous plaster work ceilings in this small "castle"; the ceilings are also hung with elegant crystal chandeliers. The castle contains Sheraton furniture, massive gilt mirrors, and fine paintings by Sir Joshua Reynolds, Sir Godfrey Kneller and other famous artists.

Sam Lord was a rich man and built the castle on the site of his plantation house at Long Bay. In addition to this, he gained control of other family property, which included Ruby in St Philip, and The Pool and Bowmanston in St John. The legend persists that Sam Lord caused the deaths of his relatives and wrecked many ships on the Cobbler's Reef, but there is no evidence with regard to his family; as to the wrecks, he was in Britain during the time when most of these wrecks occurred, between 1820 and 1821.

What does remain unknown is how he was able to afford a mansion costing approximately £30,000 in 1820. What is known is that he was a rascal who mistreated his wife, lived an immoral life, and was greatly in debt by the time of his death. In addition, he was arrested in 1817 for forgery and perjury, but he managed to have these charges dropped. On his death, the property passed to the Trollope family through his niece.

FARLEY HILL, ST PETER

In its day, this was a plantation house rivalled only by Sam Lord's Castle. It was part of the Grenade Hall estate, which was owned by the Briggs family. Sir Graham Briggs was created a baronet in 1871, and Farley Hill was extended and embellished for his marriage in 1857. During the next 20 years the garden was developed into one of the finest in the West Indies, as Sir Graham introduced many exotic trees and plants to Barbados; the indigenous Farleyens fern was discovered here.

Sir Graham was a graduate of both Codrington College and Cambridge University, a member of the House of Assembly and finally president of the Legislative Council. He was a leading supporter of Confederation in 1876, which was a proposal by Britain for the creation of a political union of the Leeward and Windward Islands, with headquarters at Barbados. The planters and merchants of Barbados opposed the scheme, fearing loss of their ancient political privileges. The workers of the island supported the idea and gave their backing to the then governor, Sir John Pope-Hennessy. Riots ensued with loss of life.

The planters, after lengthy negotiations with the Foreign Office, retained their local political privileges, which were modified, but local autonomy was permitted to continue, albeit on a restricted level and Barbados was saved from becoming a Crown Colony. Pope-Hennessy was recalled, and Sir Graham became a social outcast. He was forced to leave the island and settle on his large properties in Nevis. There he became something of a hero through his leadership and investment when Nevis was undergoing a serious financial depression. He returned to die in Barbados in 1887 at the early age of 52.

Indian River

The rivulet known as Indian River was even smaller than the Hole at Holetown. Now canalised, it is situated in the Fontabelle area west of Bridgetown, in an area formerly known as Land's End and surrounded by coconut trees and mangroves.

In 1905, along with the other tercentenary celebrations, a monument was erected near to the Indian River to commemorate the English claim to Barbados.

A sizeable Amerindian village was located here, part of a series of linked villages which covered the Bridgetown area. Today, if one walks the area, many pottery shards can be found lying on the surface; these items date from the Suazoid culture 1300–1500 AD.

WOMEN WASHING CLOTHES, INDIAN RIVER CIRCA 1898

In this photograph, four women wash clothes in the Indian River, Fontabelle. They are watched by a man wearing a jacket and a hat, in spite of the heat, and a well-dressed woman in an attractive white dress; a little girl stands in the water to watch. Two of the washer-women use stones for washing boards, a third one wrings her clothes, while a fourth one looks at the camera. In the background, and behind the lady standing on the stones, the washerwomen have laid out some of their white laundry on a bush to bleach in the sun in the traditional way.

This picture was taken after piped water had been installed in 1861, but traditional washing in a stream would have been more convenient and sociable than catching water at a stand pipe and carrying it home in several heavy buckets.

Pelican Island Quarantine Station circa 1898

This photograph is of the small offshore island known as Pelican Island, possibly because brown pelicans roosted or nested there. It was located about a quarter of a mile off Fontabelle; a little north of this was Land's End. There were two jetties off the mainland, Badley's and Carmichael's, and it was possible to wade out to the island at low tide.

The island was used as a quarantine station for ships' passengers suffering from acute infectious diseases. In addition to a house for the caretaker, there were a number of barracks for the patients, a large cauldron for boiling clothes and a mortuary.

With the opening of the Deep Water Harbour in 1961, Pelican Island was joined to the mainland and the site became a souvenir village for tourists. The present Pelican Village commemorates the lost island.

THE UNDERTAKERS, ROEBUCK STREET

Sandwiched between two undertakers is "The Old Dew Drop Inn", no doubt the purveyor of Dutch-courage to many a bereaved person. This picture, taken in Roebuck Street, shows the carriage and hearse, which would have been drawn by black horses with black plumes on their heads. For the funerals of small children, there was the heartbreaking sight of a small white pony drawing a miniature hearse and coffin. Funerals have always been expensive in Barbados.

At the time of this photograph, it would have been usual for a wake to be held the night before the funeral. It was essential for the body to be buried as quickly as possible, usually the day after the death, so the body was laid out in the coolest room and completely covered by a sheet. The night was passed by singing hymns, drinking, and taking other refreshments.

On the day of the funeral, it was important for the mourners to meet at the family residence to view the deceased for the last time, after which the lid of the coffin was screwed down. The cortege then formed up for the procession to the church; the close family in the carriage leading the hearse. Behind the hearse walked the female mourners in pairs, wearing white, followed by the men in black suits. Other men followed on bicycles; all seemed able to ride at walking pace. As in any society, the size of the procession was a mark of the deceased's standing in the community.

The normal time for funerals in Barbados was 4:00 pm. The coffin arrived and left the church feet first; the service was taken by a clergyman, there were hymns, prayers and a eulogy by a close friend. During the last hymn, the coffin was lifted by six male pall-bearers of the family of the deceased, the closest relatives lifting the head of the coffin and bearing it to the grave.

St Michael's Cathedral

Within the scope of this book the Church of England was the premier and most powerful religion on the island. It was under Governor Philip Bell, and the jurisdiction of the Bishop of London, that the Church of England came to Barbados. It was eventually the established religion of the early settlers from the old country.

In the early days this was a Godless island, with the clergy making several unsuccessful attempts to enforce observance of Sunday, while other clerics complained that the closest to God that most of the settlers came was in their profanities.

Like all religions, terrible things were done in the name of God, a biased understanding of Christian teaching, and a narrow interpretation of the Bible. The planters had the money and the Anglican Church took the planters' coin. In doing so, they denied slaves religious instruction, education, and indeed only a few brave clergymen attempted to convert the slaves to Christianity. They saw to it that any religion with differing views from theirs was given short shrift: two English Quaker ladies arrived, light years ahead of their time in their beliefs on slavery, sexual equality, etc. Legislation was rushed through to make them leave the island because they had not been resident for one year, so by law they must not hold public meetings. Another example was mob destruction of the Wesleyan Meeting House after an invitation to the planters to attend meetings with their slaves. Roman Catholics were a very small minority, particularly after the Protestant Duke of Monmouth's defeated soldiers began to arrive after the Bloody Assizes.

Even after the abolition of slavery, the Anglican church continued with pew rentals, which was obviously very divisive in terms of both race and class. It should be pointed out that pew rentals was an accepted practice in Britain at this time. Happily, good triumphed over evil and the Quakers, Wesleyans, Moravians, and many other denominations finally grew and flourished on the island.

THE INTERIOR OF ST MICHAEL'S CATHEDRAL

Built between 1660 and 1665, St Michael's Cathedral had a disastrous history. This included hurricanes, lightning strikes, disputes with contractors, bad workmanship, bulging walls, rebuilding and re-roofing. In the hurricane of 1780 the church was completely destroyed and the vestry raised £10,000 by a public lottery to rebuild it. Like the great clock tower on the East Wing of the Public Building, ambition triumphed over technology and, within two years, the huge roof span forced the hard-pressed coffers of the Cathedral to supply buttresses. Fortunately all this survived the 1831 hurricane, when the Bishop immediately opened up the Cathedral as a hospital.

The interior of the Cathedral is impressive, with a huge barrel-vaulted ceiling, and some fine details in wood and stone; but perhaps the tombs and monumental inscriptions are of most interest to a social historian.

By 1808, the Bishop of London (whose diocese, as has been mentioned before included all the British West Indian Islands) sent out instructions that Sunday Schools should be started for black children. A half-hearted attempt was made four years later to appoint a Bishop of the Caribbees; but it was not until Bishop William Hart Coleridge arrived on the island in 1825 that things really began to happen. Bishop Coleridge was a nephew of Samuel Taylor Coleridge and had been a Doctor of Divinity at Oxford, where he had graduated from Christ Church College with double first class honours. He was a brilliant choice; by 1834 the number of clergy had doubled and instead of 29 schools, there were 155. Ten thousand labourers had been converted to Christianity and baptised. Schools for the poor were built close to the churches. Some of the schools were supported by the vestry, which often fed and clothed the children as well. Soon various grants started to arrive from charitable societies in England, but this did not last for long.

St James' Parish Church

We do not have the exact dates of this church but Holetown or "The Hole" was the site of the first settlement in 1627. The first reference to St James as a parish was in 1629; it seems quite likely that the first church on consecrated ground would have been at Holetown. It was called "The Hole Church" on a map printed before 1668.

The first church would have been wooden, but it is actually recorded that a stone church was built in 1660; at that time sugar was booming and the church was prosperous. The superb old baptismal font is inscribed 1684, and the large old bell is dated 1696 and inscribed "God Bless King William". It is very much older than the American Liberty Bell.

The church was completely ruined in the 1780 hurricane, but the rebuilding was completed by 1789. It survived the 1831 hurricane, but had fallen into such bad disrepair by 1874 that major rebuilding had to be done. At that time it was extended 20 feet to the west, and the chancel enlarged.

St James looks the part of the very old church that it is, and there still exists a number of very beautiful and old gravestones and memorial plaques.

St Lucy's Parish Church circa 1907

St Lucy's Church is one of the original six parish churches on the island. It was in existence in 1629, just two years after settlement and Oldmixon describes the church in his book. He says: "The Church is dedicated to St Lucy and is built of sawed stone, very handsome and regular."

Unfortunately, the parish records begin in 1846 and are too late to give us information on the early church. The Rev. Griffith Hughes, the cleric and naturalist, is said to have taken the early records with him when he left the island in strange circumstances, after tethering his horse to a tree and boarding a ship for Britain; he said goodbye to no one.

There were some excellent clergymen on the island at the beginning of this century. Here are excerpts from a report written in 1915 by a group, The Iowa Studies in Natural History, who visited St Lucy's Church. "(Mr Bovell) took some of us on a delightful auto ride to visit the Reverend Dr Watson, Rector of St Lucy's Church. The road wound along quiet valleys with little villages until St Lucy's Church appeared with its adjoining rectory. Dr Watson is perhaps the best known of local naturalists, and is one of those rare spirits, a born naturalist with a devotion to living things of all sorts, second only to his parish and parishioners. He is an all-around naturalist of far more than ordinary ability, and his love for animals amounts to a passion. We were astonished at the size and excellent condition of his collection. A considerable part had been sent to the British Museum for identification, and part he had succeeded in identifying himself. Dr Watson has a large family and a limited income. His parochial cares are many and he serves his community with the same loving solicitude that he bestows on his collection. I was told that when famine threatened his parishioners, he went without food himself that their necessities might attempt to be supplied."

Christ Church Parish Church
Destroyed by Fire 1935

Christ Church was one of the original six parish churches, the others being St Michael, St James, St Lucy, St Peter and St Thomas.

Christ Church was built in 1629 close to the sea at Dover. It appears on Ligon's map of 1657. It was destroyed by a flood in 1669. This caused a macabre spectacle with coffins and bones sticking up out of the beach.

The second church was on a more sensible site away from the sea and overlooking Oistins. This was destroyed by the hurricane of 1780 and rebuilt after 1786. It was destroyed again by the hurricane of 1831, along with six other parish churches. The vestry minutes must have been destroyed at this time as none exist prior to 1831.

The church, which replaced the one destroyed by the hurricane of 1831, was itself destroyed by fire in 1935; the same year it was rebuilt to a new design, so there have been five churches in Christ Church.

The oldest memorial ledgers on the island are to be found in Christ Church, and are now fixed to the church walls close to the church entrance, the very oldest being kept in the Barbados Museum.

In the churchyard is the famous Chase Vault in which the coffins moved around mysteriously in spite of being deposited in a sealed vault.

St Philip's Parish Church
Destroyed by Fire 1977

The early vestry minutes are in existence for 1729–1748. The earliest record of this church is dated 1646, but absolutely nothing is known about this early building. It was severely damaged in the hurricane of 1780, as records of the damaged churches on the island are extant at Lambeth Palace. A new church was built around 1786; this too was completely demolished by the hurricane of 1831 and rebuilt in 1836. Bishop Coleridge, who made a number of sketches of the churches and chapels of ease in Barbados, made a number of drawings of St Philip's church soon after it had been rebuilt.

In 1977, the church was destroyed by fire. Although the church records were in the church at the time, they miraculously survived and are still available for study. The church has been rebuilt by voluntary subscription, but not completely restored; instead there are modern lines in the restoration, which look quite well in the old building. Very little of the fine old reredos (an ornimental screen covering a wall above the back of an altar) were saved from the fire. Originally intended for a church in South America, they were taken from a ship wreck and sold to St Philip's church by the Master of the Wrecks. Only one section of the reredos was rescued from the fire, the most valuable relic of the old church.

St Leonard's Church, St Michael
Destroyed by Fire 1982

This church was consecrated with a most impressive ceremony in 1854. It was designed to be a fashionable city church, but contained a few of the traditional building characteristics that have evolved in church building in Barbados. Somehow, it still seems architecturally out of place in Barbados.

The churchyard is very large and the elaborate funeral statuary bears testament to the wealth of its parishioners.

The church burnt to the ground in 1982. The damage was so great that the entire church has been replaced by a modern structure.

St Peter's Parish Church
Partially Destroyed by Fire 1980

The original parish church was almost certainly made of wood in 1629. It was derelict for some time, and when All Saints church was built this became the parish church for some time; a petition to divide the parish into two was never realised.

In 1665 the second church was built; this was destroyed by the hurricane of 1831 and the church was rebuilt once again in 1837. It is now a Georgian building with pediments on the front facing Church Street. Its square tower is a familiar landmark in Speightstown and it can also be seen out to sea.

St Peter's was partially destroyed by fire on 21st April 1980. Only the walls and tower survived. It has been beautifully restored at the cost of three-quarters of a million dollars.

THE SPEIGHTSTOWN JETTY CIRCA 1911

Speightstown was built on the lands of William Speight, a member of Governor Hawley's Parliament, in 1639; Hawley was the third governor of Barbados. Swann's map of circa 1640 shows it to be Spyke's Bay, and it has been pronounced that way ever since. Speightstown is 12 miles from Bridgetown. Early in the settlement of Barbados, the trade between Speightstown and Bristol was so great that it was known as Little Bristol. Schooners left Bridgetown every day at 9.30 am for Speightstown and returned to Bridgetown in the evening; the fare each way was one shilling per passenger. The alternative was a ride in a horse-drawn vehicle over rough roads.

Before the railway, virtually all the sugar and molasses from the north of the island was brought to Speightstown by mule or bullock cart. At Cockscrow Hill in St Joseph the puncheons had to be lifted off the carts and rolled up the hill by men, as the load was too heavy for the animals to draw. If the carts did not reach this hill by the time the cocks started crowing, they knew that they would not be in time to catch the schooner in Speightstown

The tower of St Peter's Church dominates Speightstown which, at the time of this photograph, was still essentially an eighteenth-century town.

The Denmark Fort, Speightstown, circa 1913

This photograph is of Denmark Fort, one of the oldest forts on the island. In this picture, the cannon and track appear in good condition, though the gunners' quarters had been turned into an almshouse; the inmates can be seen around the cannon.

The only invasion of Barbados took place in Speightstown. It came about in this way: after Cromwell's Protectorate had executed King Charles I, many of the king's supporters (or Cavaliers as they were known) emigrated to Barbados in large numbers. They were led by Humphrey Walrond, and this group usurped the Barbados government, and tyrannically fined and banished many of Cromwell's followers (who were known as the Roundheads).

Sir George Ayescue was sent out by Cromwell's Commonwealth with a fleet and 4,000 men to bring the Royalists in Barbados under control. He blockaded Carlisle Bay, which cut off supplies to the island for three months, then set about invading the island at Speightstown. He had been joined by the Barbadian planters Colonel Drax and Colonel Reynold Alleyne. The landing took place in December 1654, led by Ayescue and Alleyne, and a battle took place against the Barbadian Royalists. In spite of Colonel Alleyne being killed soon after the landing, the invaders won the day.

A Speightstown Schooner and Whaling From Speightstown

The other ships that sailed further out of these waters were the whaling ships. Among the whale species that frequented the coast of Barbados, St Vincent and the Grenadines in the early part of each year was the humpback whale. These whales were killed to extract oil from their blubber or fat layer, which encases the whole body. The flesh was eaten when fresh and considered very nourishing, the bones were used for making agricultural fertiliser and the finners, or teeth, were manufactured into coarse brooms.

The whale is easily frightened and the slightest noise from a boat would cause it to move off the feeding ground and dive deeply. The female or "cow" is very affectionate to its young, and whalers when chasing a "cow" would always try to harpoon the calf first, knowing that the mother would remain close to the calf as long as it was alive.

The capturing of a bull whale was much more difficult. The male goes at a furious rate when harpooned and sometimes, when hauled within range of the gun, will dive from 50 to 100 fathoms depth, taking all the line and escaping after doing much damage. The boat might also be drawn under water causing loss of life.

In Barbados there used to be several whaleries but, even with the improved darting gun, whaling became a lost skill. Each boat employed 14 men; the work was considered so dangerous that the men were paid wages in advance for their dependants, and later a bonus in accordance with the number of whales captured.

In 1913, 90 barrels of whale oil was extracted and sold in England at £13 to £18 per ton. American whalers used Speightstown for trading barrels of whale oil, for food, water and firewood. The Barbados whaling industry ended early this century.

The Inter-Colonial Cricket Team of 1909

The officers of the Garrison formed their own cricket club in 1805. They called it St Ann's Cricket Club. Cricket was introduced to Barbados by these officers between 1870 and 1900. It was considered a suitable game for the shaping of character in schoolboys, encouraging "civic virtue and playing the game". Harrison College and Lodge School led the way in the best tradition of the British public school. It soon became a national institution in Barbados as recreation, spectator sport, and social activity.

The early cricket clubs were Wanderers, founded in 1877 by the wealthiest planters, merchants and professionals. The Pickwick was founded in 1882 to serve the white middle classes. Their ground at Kensington Oval became the country's best venue. Wanderers, Pickwick, the Garrison and the two schools played among themselves until 1892 when the Barbados Cricket Club Committee was formed. After this the Leeward and Windward Clubs came into being for the country planters.

The next club was Spartan, the first non-white club, whose membership was derived largely from the brown middle class. Its clubhouse was located in Belleville. At that time few blacks were allowed to play at competition level even for Spartan. Empire Club was formed by the progressive Braithwaite and his friends at Bank Hall in 1915, and it was on the edge of this ground that the great Sir Frank Worrell was born ten years later, where he grew up breathing cricket.

Later new clubs were formed like Police, Carlton and YMPC. Barbados dominated West Indies cricket with Barbadians frequently claiming six or seven of the 11 places.

Combermere School

Combermere School, along with Queen's College, was probably founded earlier than any other school on the island or indeed the Commonwealth. In 1682, Henry Drax, the wealthy planter of Drax Hall, left a £2,000 endowment in perpetuity to found a free school in Bridgetown for poor children. By 1690 no trace of the money could be found, but when the Girls and Boys Central School opened in 1819 it was built on what was known as "the Free School Land". No firm evidence has been established, but Mr Drax's endowment is a possibility.

The Central Schools "originated in the anxiety felt by Lord Combermere (governor of Barbados 1817–1820) and the clergy of the island, for the establishment of a more efficient system of education among the poorer classes". At first the school was "confined to the children of white parents", and only an elementary education was provided, supported by voluntary contributions, the Legislature, and Vestries. In 1856 there was an attempt to offer higher education at the Boy's School. Between 1879–80 it was made into a second-grade school and named Combermere School. By the turn of the century it had become the preferred school of parents wishing their sons to enter commerce, banking and other related professions. Harrison College, with its emphasis on the Classics, may not have been considered relevant to their children's future.

In 1913 the headmaster was Mr G.B.R. Burton MA; there were seven members of staff, one of whom also had a degree.

HARRISON COLLEGE

Harrison College was founded in 1733 by Thomas Harrison, a wealthy Bridgetown merchant. He donated the building (which is now a Masonic Lodge near the Cathedral) and handed it over to trustees for a school for the education of poor children. By 1838 the school was in a very bad financial state: it received no money from the Legislature, and the income was very limited. As the masters were given a house in which to live free of charge, they boarded 35 private pupils, which included six girls. This enabled the school to remain solvent.

In 1871 the original building was sold and the school moved to the present location in Crumpton Street. It was at this time that a succession of very able headmasters and members of staff raised the school to a high academic standard; it was particularly distinguished for the excellence of its classical tuition. J.B. Harrison was appointed the first Island Professor of Chemistry in 1879, and he began regular science classes at the school. Mr Harrison made many valuable contributions to the sugar industry and, as a result, many of his pupils followed him into the industry and served it with distinction.

By 1911, the Reverend H. A. Dalton DD was the headmaster. There were ten members of staff all with degrees.

QUEEN'S COLLEGE CIRCA 1911

This school was founded in 1819, like Combermere School, as a Central School. At first these two schools were one institution. Boarding facilities were offered to boys, while the girls received an education in reading, arithmetic, and needlework. In 1870, following a report by the Education Commission, it was decided to reorganise the Girls' Central School, to improve its standards, and to make it a second-grade school. The school did not get off to a smooth start; before it could open the first headmistress died soon after her arrival from England. The second headmistress, also from England, believed that she was coming out to be the headmistress of a first-grade school. This was due to the enthusiasm of a member of the Education Board who had engaged her. However, this was no bad thing, as she put forward major changes to the prospectus. These obtained legislative approval, and Miss Helen Veiteh Brown became headmistress of a first-grade school. This new school opened as Queen's College in 1883, dedicated to the principle that the best possible education should be available to girls.

In 1911 Miss A. James was the headmistress (Acad. de Douai Univ. de France). There were seven other mistresses, two of whom had degrees. The book-keeping was done by Mr E.B. Skeete.

The Alexandra School, St Peter

The Alexandra school was opened in 1894 for girls of the Leeward parishes. It was named after Princess Alexandra, the then Princess of Wales, wife of the future King Edward VII.

In the 1920s it was situated opposite Arlington House in Speightstown, on a site backing the sea. It occupied two buildings of three stories and in addition to the schoolrooms, it provided accommodation for the headmistress and two assistant mistresses.

The school was such a success that it was proposed to build a similar school for the girls of the Windward parishes. In this way the plans for Codrington High School came into being.

The Alexandra School later moved from opposite Arlington to Merton House, the very old residence of the Parochial Medical Officer for St Peter.

THE URSULINE CONVENT, CIRCA 1908

The order of St Ursula was founded in 1535 by a simple Italian woman named Angela Merici. Her idea was that the Sisters should live at home and try to be an outstanding example in anything they chose to do, or whatever work they had to do. Later Angela Merici was canonised and became St Angela; however during her lifetime she had decided that she did not wish her order to be known as the "Angelines", and named it after the legendary British Princess Ursula, a patron of youth and learning.

The Ursuline's were the first order of Roman Catholic nuns to go to Canada in the "New World", a century after their founding, and to devote themselves to education. On the 5th May 1894 six Ursuline Sisters came to Barbados, and within a few days had started a school on the 12th May. This school was in a small building at the corner of Jemmott's Lane and Bay Street, with just six pupils.

This little school prospered and by 1908 the property "Linden", on Collymore Rock, was purchased for the Ursulines, and the Convent moved to this imposing building. It continued to thrive and expand but this building is the heart of the Convent, together with the beautiful Chapel which contains a magnificent altar made of malachite, a green mineral which runs in a single seam from Siberia down to Africa, and is normally used for making ornaments.

Today the Convent has 800 pupils who are taught in well maintained buildings; there is also an attractive swimming pool and other sports facilities, and the old house seen in this photograph, continues to be maintained in superb condition.

St Winifred's School circa 1922

St Winifred's School was started by Miss Jane Charlotte Seale who lived with her Aunt Annie Haney on 11th Avenue Belleville. They later moved to "Ardsley" on 9th Avenue; Miss Seale was the eldest of nine children. She started as a teacher at Grasfield School, which had been started by the three Ince sisters in 1901. That school was set in four acres and had 100 day girls and 14 boarders. By 1920 the school started to fail, partly because Codrington High School had opened in 1917 and the boarders from Grasfield School were attracted to its country setting, which diminished the income at Grasfield. When the school finally closed in 1921, 21 girls were left stranded before sitting their Junior or Senior Cambridge Examinations in July 1922. Their parents asked Miss Seale to tutor their children so that they could complete their education.

Miss Seale tried to form a syndicate to buy the old Grasfield School so that she could continue teaching, but was unable to raise the money. She enjoyed teaching so financial difficulties did not stand in her way. On the 13th September 1921, assisted by Norah Burton and Ethel Ince, she began a school with the 21 stranded girls. The school was accommodated in two rented rooms on 9th Avenue Belleville. By the next year, the school had grown and she needed more space, which she found in the schoolroom adjacent to St Cyprian's church. The new school was named in memory of Miss Seale's sister Winifred, who had died in Brooklyn, New York in 1911. Now situated at "Welbeck" Pine Hill, it stands in three acres next to Government House. Its fine school hall, its class rooms and laboratories are a tribute to Miss Seale's purpose and vision.

LODGE SCHOOL CIRCA 1913

Lodge School began as the Codrington Grammar School in 1745 in an attempt to fulfil the will of Christopher Codrington, who had left his plantations to the Society for the Propagation of the Gospel in Foreign Parts. The building took 31 years to complete and was eventually opened with 17 pupils. After many difficulties, in 1829 it was moved from the College to the chaplain's lodge on the upper estate, now Society Plantation, also part of the Codrington Bequest.

By 1850 there were 40 pupils in the school, and its purpose was to provide a secondary education for both black and white children of the middle classes. Later, the Society for the Propagation of the Gospel removed its support (in spite of Christopher Codrington's will) and it was recommended that it should become a first-grade government school.

It was between 1899 and 1931, when Mr Emtage was the headmaster, that Lodge School attained a high academic and athletic standard, becoming the great rival of Harrison College, the alma mater of its headmaster.

In 1913, at the time of this picture, Mr O de C Emtage MA was the headmaster, there were three masters, two of whom had degrees, and the mistress of the preparatory school was Miss M. Gill.

CODRINGTON HIGH SCHOOL, ST JOHN CIRCA 1918

Codrington High School was built to give the Windward parishes a school comparable to the Alexandra School in Speightstown.

The school opened on the 17th January 1917 on land owned by Codrington College. The building is beside what was known as Society Chapel just visible to the left of the picture. With its several peaked roofs, on a beautiful site overlooking a terrace, Codrington College, Consett Bay and the Atlantic, it has a stunning view. It was built at the personal expense of the Rev. A.H. Anstey, later Bishop of Trinidad. It was designed and largely built by two brothers, who were theological students at Codrington College. The desks were made by the master cabinetmaker Charles Leslie Codrington (who also built the pulpits at St John's and Christ Church).

The Rev. Clarke-Hunte was its first Committee Chairman. It was opened by the governor Sir Leslie Probyn, and the ceremony was attended by the entire Synod of Provincial Bishops who were in Barbados for the consecration of Bishop Berkeley, who had worked hard to make the idea of the school a reality.

Its first headmistress was a Barbadian and a distinguished Cambridge scholar, Miss Jessie Vinter. It was intended that the school should be a government grant-aided school like the Alexandra School. This, however, was never achieved and its struggle to survive financially was only possible through charitable gifts and its reputation as a first-class boarding school, with girls coming from the Caribbean Islands, British Guiana, Venezuela and other countries in the area.

Codrington College circa 1913

This picture shows one of the two royal palms planted by their Royal Highnesses Prince Albert Victor and Prince George. The only one to survive was planted by Prince George who became King George V.

When Christopher Codrington died in 1710, he left his plantations in Barbados to the Society for the Propagation of the Gospel, an Anglican missionary body which was started in 1701. He wished the plantation to continue in its entirety, with 300 slaves retained to work on it. His plan was that this would finance an appropriate number of professors and scholars (all under vows of poverty, chastity and obedience) to live, study, and practise there. They were to study Divinity and also "Physick and Chyrurgery" so that they could endear themselves to the common folk by doing good to their souls while taking care of their bodies. Christopher Codrington had been sent to England to be educated as a boy, and later entered All Souls College, Oxford as an undergraduate. In his will, he bequeathed his library to his college, of which he had been made a fellow.

Codrington College is situated in a romantic spot. The old plantation house became the Principal's Lodge but, due to financial problems, the college was not opened until 1745, and then Codrington's will was only fulfilled in the most limited way; it opened as a grammar school for a few sons of the elite.

It took Bishop Hart Coleridge to make it into a theological college in 1830. Under Rev. Rawle's administration there was a proposal to turn it into a school again, but he fought this and managed to improve its financial standing. In 1875, under Bishop Mitchinson, the college was affiliated to the University of Durham in England. West Indian students entered the priesthood after earning their degree there. It is the first degree-level institution in the English-speaking West Indies which survived (Queen's College Jamaica, which opened in 1873, lasted one year).

Erdiston

Erdiston was the plantation house of the Pine Plantation. Part of its grounds is on Pine Hill overlooking Belleville. The Pine Plantation house was built in 1756 by William Barwick. It was the town house of Sir Graham Briggs between 1864 and 1887, used when he was not overseas or in residence at Farley Hill.

Erdiston subsequently became the home of Mr Sam Manning, who had the idea of designing a suburb of Bridgetown, laid out in avenues and planted with stately cabbage palms. This he called Belleville.

Mr Manning offered the site for Queen's College, later the government deemed the site unsatisfactory but subsequently acquired Erdiston from the Manning estate. It remained empty for many years, but in 1948 it opened as a teacher training college for primary school teachers. Later it was expanded to include the Erdiston model primary school.

Early students at the training college were allocated parts of the extensive gardens for which they were responsible. This offered them an extra-curricular activity, and no doubt cut down on the gardener's wages.

The Government Industrial School for Boys

In 1883 a reformatory and industrial school for boys was opened at Dodds. By 1910 the Legislature gave the necessary sanction for the establishment of a girls' reformatory which subsequently opened as "Summervale". In addition to being corrective centres, these schools attempted to teach the children a useful trade so that they could earn a living when they were released.

These schools were residential, and run in a similar way to a prison. In the middle of the picture the boys are drawn up in the court yard and dressed like convicts. It can be assumed that they had a strictly regimented routine with corrective measures, which would have included corporal punishment.

It was in an experimental plot at Dodds that J.B. Pilgrim reported a type of "grass" similar to young sugar cane growing here, which subsequently proved that cane could seed.

THE BASKET SELLER

In this picture, a country boy poses in the photographic studio of Mr Parkinson with a variety of split cane baskets. Basket making was practised in Barbados from the time of early settlement. The tradition was strong in both Britain and Africa.

Many types of baskets were made, each quite distinctive, using cabbage cope, palm fronds, split canes, and gully vines for dung baskets. The dung basket is still used today, but they were in great demand in the second half of the seventeenth century; cultivation had so exhausted the soil that farm yard manure was needed by the planters. Small farmers whose land was in parts of the island unsuitable for sugar, turned to dung farming. This dung was sold to the plantations, but as the planters began to keep more livestock themselves, the dung farmers were forced out of business.

HERBERT

This picture of Herbert is posed and was taken in a studio. Herbert was well known as a fiddler in Bridgetown. He could only play one tune, but would sing different songs to the accompaniment of this tune. He was befriended by Mr and Mrs Hill of Fontabelle, who gave him three meals a day, and in whose boat house he lived for many years, sleeping in a coil of rope covered by a sail. On the death of this couple, he moved on to a Mr Hassel who continued to look after him until his death.

For "a Sixpence" or 12 cents Herbert would play his fiddle and sing, his two most popular songs being: "The Thing You Used To Do, Don't Do It Anymore", and "A Little More Oil In Your Lamp To Keep It Burning Till The Break Of Day". This is a tribute to Herbert. May the memory of the pleasure he gave so many people live on.

A Huckster

This elderly hawker is selling horn yams. She is wearing a head tie and a pad, on which is placed the heavy wooden tray filled with yams. These yams are completely unlike the "yams" of the United States, which are known on the island as sweet potatoes. In Allsopp's *Dictionary of Caribbean English Usage,* the word "yam" is used in West and Central Africa to mean "meat" or "food" or "to eat". On top of all this is a crocus bag in which she kept her knife and other small articles. If it rained, she would push one corner of the crocus bag into the other and wear it on her head as a hood, with the rest of the bag protecting her back from the rain. Her money would be kept tied securely around her waist in a cloth bag which often contained a lucky "horse eye", a large brown bean, an African talisman, found on the beach at Cattlewash. Washed across the Atlantic from Africa, they must have been found with delight by the early slaves. They are plentiful on the beaches of the Côte d'Ivoire where they are reputedly washed down from the rivers in Mali.

Having bought these yams from a plantation or a small farmer, or grown them herself, this elderly lady would have had to walk some distance with her heavy load. Here she appears to be in a suburb of Bridgetown.

THE MAUBY VENDOR

This mauby vendor could direct a stream of mauby from the container on her head straight into a foaming tot. This slightly bitter drink is made from the bark of the mauby tree (Columbrina elliptica) and is still popular on the island. It has the reputation of having some unspecified medicinal benefit – probably because children rarely like it, so it must be good for them. The bark is boiled with spices in water, then strained and sugared to taste.

The mauby tree does not grow well in Barbados; the main suppliers of the bark are the Dominican Republic and Haiti. The early indentured labourers on the island were given a drink called "mobbie" as part of their diet, but this was an entirely different drink made from sweet potatoes, and probably fermented in the Amerindian tradition.

FOUR VENDORS WITH TRAYS

In this posed photograph the four ladies are all selling different things. From the left there is the "Sweetie Lady", whose immaculate tray would have displayed coconut sugar cakes in three colours, peanut cakes both white and transparent (known as glassies), twisted peppermint sticks decorated with little bits of yellow and red boiled sugar, blocks of the same peppermints known as "comfits", transparent boiled sugar in yellow and red cut in the shape of roosters and stuck on the mid rib of coconut leaves, and opaque triangular ginger cakes. All this would be covered by a starched snow white cloth. Unlike the attitude on many other West Indian islands, these sweets were considered completely hygienic and were consumed by children of every class on the island, as they had been enjoyed by their parents and grandparents.

The lady in the doorway was probably selling flat slabs of pone. In November she would sell conkies wrapped in banana leaves and steamed. The lady on the far right was probably selling flat corn biscuits, coconut bread and cakes (there appears to be some paper bags on the tray waiting to be filled).

The seated lady has two "fancy baskets", from which she would sell ribbons, lace, tape, shoelaces, buttons, hooks and eyes, threads, needles and pins; at Christmas time she would also sell Christmas cards. There is a pair of scissors hanging from her waist. Notice her well-made dress and hat in contrast to the clothes and head ties of the other three ladies. The ladies with "fancy baskets" were very respectable and would not carry their wares on their heads. They were often invited into houses to see the sewing in progress and in order to supply the right trimmings. These ladies considered themselves superior to hucksters.

Ginning Cotton circa 1920

Here, well-dressed women are employed for the delicate job of ginning cotton. Ginning removed the cottonseeds and produced cotton lint, which would be baled and exported; the seeds would be pressed for cottonseed oil. Notice that these ladies wear hats instead of head ties, denoting their superior status and earnings.

Cotton has been grown on the island since the time of the early settlers; peak production was reached at the end of the eighteenth century. This boom was caused by demand resulting from the Industrial Revolution. Annual exports of cotton from Barbados reached over £2,000,000 in the late 1780s. In the early eighteenth century, a Barbadian submitted a patent claim for the invention of a cotton-ginning machine; this was some years before the Eli Whitney cotton gin patented in the USA.

The Cotton Factory was opened in 1905 to replace the Cotton Central Committee, which had been responsible for the ginning, baling and shipping of cotton. As with tobacco, the rapid and large-scale production of cotton in the United States outstripped Barbados, and the industry went into decline.

MINING MANJACK

Manjack is bitumen-rich coal found mostly in the Scotland District. This thick black substance was known from the days of the early settlers, who used it like pitch to caulk boats. Later, in the days of boiling-houses on the plantations, it was mixed with bagasse as fuel for furnaces to boil the tayches of syrup. In 1895 it was mined in large quantities and exported for use in the manufacture of paint, varnish, asphalt paving and early gramophone records.

The first manjack mines were opened in January, 1896 on the College Estate. There were also mines at Spring Vale and Bruce Vale in St Andrew. About 35 men and boys and ten women were employed in these mines; the owner was R.H. Emtage. It is surmised that manjack deposits extend under the coral in all parts of the island.

Manjack was available in three grades, ranging in price from $15 to $25 per 2,000 pounds. During the First World War some of it was used as a fuel for trains. Synthetic compounds eventually replaced manjack, hence its decline; the mining of manjack stopped in 1920.

THE SPECULATOR

This is a posed picture, the speculator with his notebook recording the deal, the other curious people roped in for the photograph. People in country villages looked forward to the visit of the speculator, who was regarded as a well-travelled man, with news of Bridgetown and outlying villages. Speculators would buy cattle and pigs and move them on for sale to people according to their needs; some people wanted to breed, or to slaughter, often people with small children in a family would be looking for a milch cow.

The speculator always expected to make money on these deals and usually did. Many successful Barbadian families of both races can trace their wealth to a speculator antecedent.

RED LEG FISHERMEN AT MARTIN'S BAY CIRCA 1910

A group of poor white fishermen, some wearing tunics made of old sugar bags (crocus bags) show off the tools of their trade: nets for casting for fray or sprats, a rod for catching small fish like jacks, to eat or use for bait when open-sea fishing for larger fish such as bonito or barracuda.

Generations of these poor white fisherfolk, living in villages which dotted the coastline of St Lucy, St John, St Philip and Christ Church, have used the sea to provide themselves and their families with a subsistence existence. Malnutrition, inbreeding and hookworm infestation greatly debilitated them and they had a much shorter life span than other Barbadians. A Rockefeller Foundation grant identified the hookworm infestation, but it was years before money was forthcoming for treatment.

After the displacement of the white labourers by the black slaves, many emigrated to other West Indian islands or the Carolinas. Those who remained joined the militia and were given a couple of acres on plantations to provided for themselves and help the planters fulfil their quota of volunteers. This way the planters could keep more effective workers on the plantation. The main function of the militia was to act as a deterrent to slave rebellions. After emancipation, the militia was disbanded and the white labourers had to leave the plantations and they sank even lower in the social scale. Though they were despised, efforts were made to help them through poor relief, education, and assisted emigration. With increased social mobility their numbers decreased and finally through inter-marriage they have now almost disappeared.

Joe's River

Joe's River is a stream which drains the hilly region of St Joseph. The Constitution River and Joe's River are the only "rivers" in Barbados. Joe's River runs into the sea between Bathsheba and Cattlewash. A bridge which was built at the time of the railway still exists over this river. In old maps it is sometimes called St Joseph's River.

The Weir at Joe's River

Joe's River could be reduced to a trickle in the dry season; in the wet season it could be quite spectacular. When it was particularly rainy, huge fans of brown silt would spread out into the blue Atlantic at both Bathsheba and Cattlewash. Crayfish, eels and mussels have been caught in the river and at the time of this photograph they were still in reasonable supply.

Washing Day In The Country

In this photograph taken by Mr Cooper in 1891, a telling commentary emerges on the conditions of the rural labourers in nineteenth century Barbados. These small wooden shacks located cheek by jowl relate closely to the late eighteenth century houses depicted in prints and drawings. Built from bits of second hand wood, this house appears to bear testimony to being disassembled and reassembled more than once, which would have been the lot of the owner as his own "chattel", to be moved at the will of the plantation for whatever reason, or in some cases the labourer may have wished to move on to work at another plantation for better conditions or wages, though there was a fine to try to prevent this.

The composition of the picture is also interesting and shows an "insider's" view demonstrated by the photographer. It captures the impermanence of life on rented land, and it shows us something of the standard of personal cleanliness which was achieved by the owner. A washing tub and a scrubbing board (or "juking board") is balanced on a bucket in the foreground. The dazzling white clothes lie bleaching in the sun in the traditional way. A shoeless young man steps from the side of the house by a type of sisal plant with its flowering "may pole". His gait and pristine shirt and felt hat tell us that he may be down but not out.

A Chattel House, Martin's Bay, circa 1930

Nothing perhaps is more indicative of a Barbadian landscape than a chattel house. Early watercolours suggest that these wooden structures made their first appearance in the late-eighteenth century. Their balanced design borrowed concepts of harmony from the prevailing Georgian style of architecture then used on the island.

After emancipation, ex-slaves were moved from the traditional slave quarters or "Negro yards" of the plantations to marginal lands, usually on the perimeter of the plantation. These lands continued to be owned by the plantation, a device to ensure a constant supply of labour, and were rented to individual workers, who could be evicted at short notice if, for any reason, they and the plantation management had a disagreement. Faced with this dilemma, the chattel house provided the tenant with an ideal solution; it could be dismantled, moved and reassembled elsewhere.

So popular did this type of housing become that more elaborate versions were built by urban families, particularly during the period of the construction of the Panama Canal, with funds saved and sent back to the island.

Imported timber came in lengths from 12 to 24 feet in even numbers; chattel houses are symmetrical and use these lengths.

The Stand Pipe Above Consett Bay

When piped water was introduced into Barbados in 1861, 400 standard pipes were installed, giving free water to the population. The name "stand pipe" is an abbreviation of "standard pipe". The "standard" was the large metal cylinder to which the faucet was attached; the more modern pipes were set in cement. Galvanised buckets and other containers were used to transport the water home from the pipe, usually on a woman's head; at home it was stored in large barrels or drums. The grace and rhythm with which these women carried these heavy buckets on their heads can still be seen in Africa.

The stand pipe served the same social purpose as wells, streams and riverbanks in other cultures; it too became the centre of village gossip, news, love affairs, and feuds. The stand pipe was always a source of great pleasure for children, playing the numerous water games known to every child; but perhaps the stand-pipe jokes, which led to the "stand pipe laugh", is what they are best remembered for.

BATHSHEBA FLYING FISH FLEET WITH SAILS

Here the flying fish boats return to Tent Bay after a day of fishing. They left about 4:00 am and returned about 4:00 pm. Quite often, while attempting to re-enter the Channel at high tide they would capsize and lose their entire catch. Fishing boats with sails were quite usual until 1955 when hurricane Janet destroyed much of the sail boat fleet, after which sails were gradually replaced by motor engines.

Flying fish can soar through the air at speeds of 55 kilometres per hour, and for as long as 13 seconds at a stretch. Propelled by its tail fin, the flying fish leaps from the water and glides considerable distances using its two pectoral and two ventral fins. They return to the water when their fins dry out.

The flying-fish season is from December to June. Although there are 13 species of flying fish in Barbadian waters, the entire industry fishes one species only, *Etinurdichthys affinis*. They are sometimes caught with a gill net as they swim in shoals. They are attracted to floating objects to which they attach their orange eggs, which do not float. Another method that was used was to wait until a few flying fish rose out of the water; the sails and mast were then lowered and the boat allowed to drift. A bag of pounded rotten fish was lowered over the stern of the boat, and the fish oil that was released made the water calm and attracted the fish which were simply scooped out of the water with landing nets. Boats have been known to sink from overloading.

When spawning, the fish can be scooped out of the water with a dip net. Flying fish probably only live for a year or two in natural circumstances. Barbados has been called the "Land of the Flying Fish". The early settlers called them Barbados Pigeons.

Cattlewash circa 1890

A favourite place for rest, recreation and recuperation, it was quieter than Bathsheba, without a railway station or fishing fleet. It probably got its name from the cattle which roamed freely up and down the beach.

This wild stretch of coastline on the east coast is dear to the hearts of all Barbadians. When you slip over the rim of Hackleton's Cliff, a big dark blue surf crashes in on a crescent of sand and the view runs through three parishes north to Pico Teneriffe. Past Cattlewash, the dry cracked face of Napoleon is outlined by Chalky Mount. Round Rock looks like a huge black marble washed up by some primeval tide. Jagged teeth of rock take the full force of the big Atlantic breakers. Green hills back the beach, long vines of goats foot with mauve flowers grow out onto the baking sand, but the air is fresh and salty with spray that looks like Champagne in the hot midday sun. This area must be preserved because its full beauty and significance can only be appreciated by Barbadians, who consider it another world.

At the time of this photograph, the area was just being opened up by the railway, and the first of the wooden bay houses were being erected.

Poor Barbadians circa 1890

There was much poverty in Barbados. In this photograph, poor blacks and whites are living together on the east coast, the poor blacks showing many kindnesses to the whites (despite their racial arrogance), whom they recognised as unable to cope with their lives of destitution in the tropics.

During a particularly harsh drought and famine in 1847, the poor whites came down from the Scotland Hills to pick “fat porks” (a sour wild fruit). When they had depleted the ripe ones, they boiled up the green ones in an attempt to make soup. They also made grey gaulin soup from the herons that inhabited the ponds and swamps of the east coast.

Emancipation was harsh on the poor whites, over 8,000 of them being ejected from the plantations where they had previously worked. Completely marginalised, many died from starvation, and the local government initiated an emigration scheme to the neighbouring islands of St Vincent, Bequia and Grenada in an effort to save them. Poor blacks, on the other hand, continued to be employed by the plantations and faced the prospect of more hard labour and low wages. Escape from the vicious cycle of poverty was possible for both blacks and whites only through education or migration.

BARBADIAN CHILDREN CIRCA 1900

This book is not a tribute to the rich elite of Barbados, the absentee landlords, the people who sent their children "home" to school, or their money "away" for better and safer interest rates and security. Nor is it about the "Johnnies-come-lately", building on foundations laid by old families of Barbadians of both colours, with blood, sweat, and tears.

This book is about all of the people who came to Barbados (mostly against their will) almost 400 years ago. The early white settlers roasting in the midday sun as labourers, while their features were slowly eaten away by skin cancer, in spite of their facemasks; subsisting on food they had never seen or tasted before, living in close proximity with a race of people they had never seen in the old country. Together they survived the terrible droughts, the furious hurricanes and devastating fires. Forced to share, observe and learn from each other, they formed a common culture. It is about the people who made the physical and spiritual journey to climb up from "under the cliff".

Barbadian Children circa 1900

This book is about all of the displaced people who survived a terrible physical and mental journey. The ancestors of these children came from many West African countries and tribes, all with distinct languages and at first could scarcely communicate among themselves. They triumphed against the odds to produce generations of strong and healthy children. It is about the children in the third gangs, giving their few cents wages each week to parents to help to feed a family.

These are the children who studied in chattel houses by candles and oil lamps to pass examinations set in a country they had never seen and barely understood; who passed these examinations with distinction, to take their places at elite universities, and enter elite professions. They did not become so elitest that they forgot their own people, they returned to their island as doctors and lawyers, entered politics and lifted their people up with them in every aspect of life.

By chance they arrived and settled on a beautiful island, by hard work and determination they have made it their own. Now people from "away" are very welcome to come and share it for a memorable week or two of their lives, but this land is ours and every square inch should remain ours forever.

BIBLIOGRAPHY

A–Z of Barbados Heritage, Henry Fraser, Sean Carrington, Addinton Forde, John Gilmore, Heinemann Publishers (Caribbean) Ltd, Jamaica, 1990

Historic Bridgetown, Warren Alleyne, The Barbados National Trust, 1978.

The Garrison and its Buildings, Warren Alleyne and Jill Sheppard, MacMillan Caribbean, London, 1990

The Redlegs of Barbados, Jill Sheppard, Kto Press, New York, 1977

Glimpses of Old Barbados, Edward A. Stoute S.C.M, The Barbados National Trust, 1986.

A History of Barbados, Ronald Tree, Rupert Hart-Davies Ltd., London, 1972

Historic Churches of Barbados, Barbara Hill, Art Heritage Publications, Barbados, 1984.

The Civilised Island of Barbados, Karl Watson, Caribbean Graphic Production Ltd, Barbados, 1979

A Brief History of Barbados, Karl Watson, Hansib Caribbean, London, 1997

Barbados Illustrated, Cave Shepherd & Co., 1911

Da Costa's Barbados Illustrated, DaCosta & Co., 1911

The History of Sugar, Noel Deerr, 2 Vols., London, 1949- 1950

Handbook of Barbados, E Goulburn Sinckler, Duckworth & Co., London, 1913.

Encyclopedia Britannica, 1975

Shilstone Memorial Library, Train Section, Barbados Museum Papers